The Work Of The People

Liturgical Aids

John H. Will

CSS Publishing Company, Inc., Lima, Ohio

THE WORK OF THE PEOPLE

Copyright © 2004 by
CSS Publishing Company, Inc.
Lima, Ohio

The original purchaser may photocopy material in this publication for use as it was intended (i.e., worship material for worship use; educational material for classroom use; dramatic material for staging or production). No additional permission is required from the publisher for such copying by the original purchaser only. Inquiries should be addressed to: Permissions, CSS Publishing Company, Inc., P.O. Box 4503, Lima, Ohio 45802-4503.

Scripture quotations are from the *New Revised Standard Version of the Bible*, copyright 1989 by the Division of Christian Education of the National Council of the Churches of Christ in the USA. Used by permission.

Library of Congress Cataloging-in-Publication Data

Will, John H. (John Harold), 1935-
   The work of the people : liturgical aids / John H. Will.
      p. cm.
Includes bibliographical references.
   ISBN 0-7880-2301-2 (pbk. : alk. paper)
   1. Public worship. 2. Liturgies. 3. Worship programs. I. Title.
BV10.3.W55 2003
264—dc22

2003019428

For more information about CSS Publishing Company resources, visit our website at www.csspub.com or e-mail us at custserv@csspub.com or call (800) 241-4056.

ISBN 0-7880-2301-2　　　　　　　　　　　　　　　　PRINTED IN U.S.A.

*This labor of love is
dedicated to those saints
who through the years
have shaped and deepened
my appreciation of worship.*

Table Of Contents

Acknowledgments	9
Introduction	11
Advent/Opportunity *Luke 3:7-18; Isaiah 12:2-6*	13
After Christmas *Luke 2:21-38*	16
Blessedness/Trust *Luke 6:17-26; Jeremiah 17:5-10*	19
Blindness/Seeing *Mark 10:46-52; Isaiah 42:14-20*	22
Bread *John 6:24-35; Ephesians 4:7, 11-16*	25
Challenge *1 Samuel 17:32-46a, 48-50a*	28
Choosing *Joshua 24:1-3a, 14-25; Amos 5:21-24*	31
Chosen *Isaiah 6:1-8; Luke 5:1-11*	34
Connectedness *Luke 24:44-53; Ephesians 1:17-23*	37
Costly Grace *Luke 14:25-35; Philemon 1-21*	40
Dancing With God *2 Samuel 6:1-5, 11-19*	43
Deafness/Hearing *Mark 7:31-37; Isaiah 35:4-7a*	46
Depth Of Devotion *Mark 7:1-9, 14-15, 21-23; James 1:22-27*	49
Dwelling Place *2 Samuel 7:1-14, 17*	52
Easter *Matthew 28:1-10; Romans 6:3-11*	55

Father   58
   Ephesians 6:1-4
Forgiveness   61
   Matthew 18:21-35
Freedom   64
   James 1:25; Romans 13:8-14a
Friend   67
   John 15:9-17
Garments   70
   Ephesians 4:25—5:2; John 6:35, 41-51
Giving/Greed   73
   Mark 12:41-44; Matthew 27:3-10
Glory   76
   2 Corinthians 4:3-6; Mark 8:27-33; 9:2-9
God's Family   79
   Ephesians 3:14-19; John 17:6-19
Hospitality   82
   Hebrews 13:1-8, 15-16; Luke 14:1, 7-14
Living Stones   85
   1 Peter 2:4-6; Matthew 16:13-20
Losing Equals Living   88
   Mark 8:31-35; Proverbs 1:20-33
Mother/Family   91
   John 13:31-35; 1 Corinthians 13:4-8a, 13
New Year/New Beginnings   94
   Isaiah 43:15-21; 2 Corinthians 5:16-21
Open Hands   97
   Luke 7:36—8:3
Palm Sunday   100
   John 12:12-19
Peace   104
   John 14:23-29; 2 Corinthians 4:13-18
Power   107
   John 6:56-69; Ephesians 6:10-17
Pruning   110
   John 15:1-8; 1 John 4:16b-21
Responsibility   113
   James 1:23-25; Luke 10:25-37

The Risen Christ	116
John 21:1-19	
Sabbath	119
Isaiah 58:9b-14; Luke 13:10-17	
Saints	122
John 6:20-31	
Second Sunday Of Easter	125
Romans 10:14-18; John 20:19-31	
A Servant Cleansing	128
John 13:1-9; Matthew 27:15-26	
Sharing	131
Luke 16:19-31; 1 Timothy 6:6-11, 17-19	
Shepherd	134
John 10:11-18	
Songs Of The Season/Advent	137
Luke 1:39-56; Micah 5:2-5a	
Spirit Of Truth	140
John 14:8-17, 25-27; Romans 8:14-17	
Spiritual Gifts/One Body	143
1 Corinthians 12:1-11; John 2:1-11	
Stewardship	146
Matthew 25:14-30; 2 Corinthians 9:5-15	
Storms	149
Matthew 14:22-33	
Thanksgiving	152
Deuteronomy 26:1-11; John 6:25-35	
Things Of First Importance	155
Mark 12:28-34; Hosea 6:1-6	
This Earthly Life	159
Deuteronomy 34:1-12; Romans 14:7-9	
Transfiguration/Fully Awake	163
Luke 9:28-36; Exodus 34:29-35	
Unity In Christ	166
Ephesians 4:1-6, 15-16; John 17:20-24	
Willingly	169
Luke 9:51-62; Galatians 5:1, 13-14	
Scripture References	173

Acknowledgments

Our lives thrive on encouragement. Many a project would never see the light of day unless there surfaced first that word of beckoning, that calm but assertive, "Do it!" — that urging of the spirit.

This offering owes its impetus to five years of pastoral ministry at the United Church of Christ in Sun City, California. This "retirement" congregation, full of veterans of the faith, was nonetheless ever willing to experiment with new and fresh forms of liturgy. They, moreover, prized having it all "written down" in the worship bulletin, so that it was not only a matter of the ear but also of the eye — and then of the mind and heart in retrospect. This certainly prompted a thorough preparation each and every Sunday, with ample words of critique, most of which were happily in the affirmative. Thus, many thanks for a continual feeding of my spirit and the prompting of talents during that very productive time of ministry.

Also, there was that quiet but never-failing encouragement coming from my helpmate Han. This has continued for better than 44 years — and is always there — even to the many constructive suggestions for this manuscript and the meticulous proofing of it. A loving daughter Elisa also gave these pages a thorough once-over, not without many comments that were valued and incorporated into the finished product. I continue to count on the many blessings of our love.

Introduction

Liturgy, as derived from the Greek, means literally "the work of the people." Thus, in Christian worship the liturgy ought to elicit the full participation of the people of God, that is, all those gathered for worship in that place.

To achieve this end, within the worship service there should be ample opportunity for all to participate, not merely in passive mode but in active. Moreover, the liturgy should be in the language of the people and of a structure that makes for reading in unison. Therefore, although some of the readings in the liturgical aids that follow are shown as responsive readings (i.e., calls to worship and psalter readings), many of the others may be included in the worship service as readings by the entire congregation rather than by a single individual. This is to be encouraged and may be varied from week to week.

Rather than follow the order of the liturgical year, the offerings included are by theme, with appropriate scripture references added as possible texts for homilies on that theme. As you will note, every effort is made throughout the liturgy to link each part to the whole. Thus will the worship, it is hoped, be integral — and will lead not only to praise and celebration but to reflection and insight on the theme for the day. Sufficient themes are included for the 52 Sundays of a year.

May your congregation indeed find liturgy to be an enlivening work of the people, the whole people of God!

Advent/Opportunity

Luke 3:7-18
Isaiah 12:2-6

Call to Worship
There was one who came to prepare the way.
Yes, John acknowledged this to be his role.
His message, "Repent," was a message of hope.
"Repent" indeed is one of the loveliest words in our language.
We come to incorporate it into our worship today.
Let us find here an opportunity to grow in our faith.

Invocation
God, we thank you for introducing us properly to the coming of your Son. You know that the way must be readied, else we miss the significance of his coming. For the danger is that we shall not recognize him, nor the import of the message he brings. Thus, you sent your messenger John to "level" with us: Get your act together. Personally admit your need. Ready yourself to welcome a Savior into your life, one who can lift you from ever-changing patterns of error and wrongdoing onto the solid ground of truth. We use our worship today, Lord, to look at need, that our admission of need become opportunity. Help us in this task, we pray. Guide us in your way. Amen.

Call to Confession
We can easily party our way through this season and find it past before we have learned its lesson. Since the lesson is good news, divine opportunity placed before each, why would we ever consciously want to bypass its significance for our lives? Indeed, we had best take another look at the season — and at our need — that we might better see how the two intersect.

Prayer of Confession
Dear God, your servant John admonished us to probe deep within ourselves — that we clearly see wherein we fall short, acknowledge our need, and turn ourselves toward you — this in expectation of the good that you stand ready to bestow on each of us. Yet many of the activities of this season would focus our attention elsewhere. Besides, we are loathe to admit need; we'd rather not have to acknowledge our dependence upon another, even though that other showers us with good. Seize us gently but firmly, we pray, and cause us to delve deep into the spirit, our spirit. Moreover, help us then to discern what your Spirit would say to ours, for in truth you have a joyful message to share with us. Prepare us so to comprehend its wonder and its inclusiveness. This through Christ, the Revealer of your love to all. Amen.

Words of Assurance
Those who turn to God, who acknowledge need and dependence, there find One who is full of mercy and compassion, One who cares for us as a shepherd tenderly cares for his sheep. This great Keeper of the sheep will keep us from stumbling, and will lift before us opportunity, a path of righteousness, great joy, and peace, that leads to life, life as only God can bestow.
Thanks be to God for a care that never fades nor falters but is always there — for us.

Psalter Reading (from Psalm 30)
Sing praises to the Lord, O you his faithful ones, and give thanks to his holy name.
For his anger is but for a moment; his favor is for a lifetime.
Weeping may linger for the night, but joy comes in the morning.
As for me, I said in my prosperity, "I shall never be moved."
By your favor, O Lord, you had established me as a strong mountain; you hid your face; I was dismayed.
To you, O Lord, I cried, and to the Lord I made supplication.
"What profit is there in my death, if I go down to the Pit? Will the dust praise you? Will it tell of your faithfulness?
Hear, O Lord, and be gracious to me! O Lord, be my helper!"

You have turned my mourning into dancing; you have taken off my sackcloth and clothed me with joy.
So will my soul praise you and not be silent. O Lord my God, I will give thanks to you forever.

Offering Sentences
Let us bear fruits worthy of repentance. Let our offerings speak to the change, the radical change, that has taken place in our lives — that change brought about by the promise of Jesus with us — our hope for today, tomorrow, and forever. Never have we known greater opportunity for this life. How will we now express this in gifts of thanksgiving?

Prayer of Dedication
Each of these offerings, O Lord, is precious in your sight. For it represents the dedication, the loyalty, and the love of one of your servants. Taken together, they are the gifts of your people in this place. Use them now, according to your Spirit's prompting, to lead still others into that joyous experience of newness of life in your name. Touch with your love, we pray, many who otherwise would feel neglected and left out — for indeed we know that you came for all. Amen.

Benediction
The time is drawing near. This is the opportune time. A great celebration lies ahead! Let us prepare ourselves that we savor fully its significance for us and for all the world. Come, Lord Jesus; we await your birthing in us. Amen.

After Christmas

Luke 2:21-38

Call to Worship
We've been there. We've had our Christmas. What now?
Were you not inspired? Did you not hear the angels sing?
Oh, it was okay. I got a good feeling. What was it supposed to do?
The love it brought should also make us want to love.
You mean every day? In a new kind of way? Is that possible?
That is why Christ came — to show us the way. And, yes, every day!
Well, this is a new day. Perhaps we can begin right now.
Yes, let our worship begin to express what Christmas has taught.

Invocation
Thank you, God, that Christmas is not just a day; it is an attitude, a whole new way of living. It is living in your presence, O God, for you are with us, with us always — to counsel, to guide, but most important of all, to demonstrate your love to us over and over again. Then maybe, just maybe one of these days, we will learn how to appropriate it fully into our lives, and so come to know the peace that you would give. In the meantime, we sing your praise with songs from the heart, and we thank you for thinking so highly of us that you have gifted us so. We worship you, Lord God. Christmas has again opened our eyes. Amen.

A Litany for After Christmas Day
The gifts have been unwrapped, but the song remains in our heart.
Joy in our lives and joy to the world, O God.
The festive holiday meal has long since disappeared, but you, Lord, promise to feed us each day and with abundance.
Joy in our lives and joy to the world, O God.
Family has come and gone, but their love abides with us still. How we need that love!
Joy in our lives and joy to the world, O God.

Twinkling lights on Christmas displays are fewer each night, yet lighting our way with ever-growing intensity is the light of Christ.
Joy in our lives and joy to the world, O God.
The tree will soon be dismantled; the ornaments packed away. The message of Christmas, however, will never be dismantled, nor packed away. It stands in full view as the hope of all ages.
Joy in our lives and joy to the world, O God.
Special good works of the season have been accomplished. We feel good about that. Yet our year-long serving of the Christ has just begun.
Joy in our lives and joy to the world, O God.
One day, one holy day, is now a memory. Its influence on us, though, is real and powerful; and we shall be renewed, our faith tells us, each time we gather for worship in his name.
Joy in our lives and joy to the world, O God. The work of Christmas has just begun. Amen.

Psalter Reading (from Psalm 96)

O sing to the Lord a new song; sing to the Lord, all the earth.
Sing to the Lord, bless his name; tell of his salvation from day to day.
Declare his glory among the nations, his marvelous works among all peoples.
For great is the Lord, and greatly to be praised; he is to be revered above all gods.
Honor and strength are before him; strength and beauty are in his sanctuary.
Ascribe to the Lord, O families of the peoples, ascribe to the Lord glory and strength.
Ascribe to the Lord the glory due his name; bring an offering, and come into his courts.
Worship the Lord in holy splendor; bow down before him, all the earth.

Offering Sentences
With all of our spending at Christmas, is there anything left for a gift to the child? Our faith is here put to the test, for the child, it turns out, is *any* of these who are his brothers and sisters. How will we treat the least of these now that all of the holiday appeals are over and a new year is about to begin? Our offerings are the first sure indicator of Christmas joy come true. Let us present them as an act of worship and as our thanksgiving to God.

Prayer of Dedication
May the joy of Christ in our hearts awaken us, O God, to those very practical ways in which we can serve the neighbor in need. Continue to remind us, we pray, that love can never be confined to word alone but must express itself in deed. May these offerings facilitate deeds of love in many a different setting, that not only our gifts but our lives be involved in building communities of faith and whole peoples in peace. This we ask in the name of the newborn, Jesus the Christ. Amen.

Benediction
We have once again enjoyed the wonder, the majesty, and the gifts of Christmas. Now it is time to roll up our sleeves and get on with the work of Christmas, as we share its message and its mercy with all who hunger and thirst, that all of us be filled. Amen!

Blessedness/Trust

Luke 6:17-26
Jeremiah 17:5-10

Call to Worship
It is not what we have but who we are that counts.
We are children of the living God.
We are disciples of the Lord Jesus Christ.
We are members of the household of faith.
So do we affirm our trust in the Author and Redeemer of life.
So do we gather now to worship God, an act that further confirms our identity.

Invocation
God, we are led to a life of service by One who himself came to serve. It is by giving ourselves away in your name that we find our greatest joy. Not only would we learn this, but ask to be inspired by your Spirit to follow through — that we put into practice what we know to be true. Thus can our whole life be one grand experience of our love for you and for neighbor, friend, and stranger. Though we have much learning and practicing left to do, we trust that your caring, your patience, and your mercy will indeed be with us as we move forward — to that level of living worthy of your blessing and benediction. Praise be to you, O God, for example and resources and motivating Spirit. We pray in Jesus' name, who brings all to fulfillment. Amen.

Call to Confession
We reach a certain level, whether that be of trust or service or right living, and at that point we say, "Enough." Though this may be far from the complete giving of self that Christ displayed, we balk at any further conditioning of body, mind, and spirit. And there it is that we stagnate. Let us pray that God shake us loose — for further growth, for a greater measure of service that only a true and full reliance on God can inspire.

Prayer of Confession
It seems, O God, that we are content with only a little, when you would give us much. We need to get our priorities aright, for inevitably these play mightily upon our relationship with you. What we want a lot of — is short-lived; it does not last for long. It is material, and rusts and erodes, until nothing is left. What truly endures — why, that we hardly recognize, and fail to pursue. Yet that comes to us as life, life eternal, and wondrously it is a gift from your hand to each of us. Forgive us this shortsightedness of spirit that limits us with little. Enable us to reach out to embrace the fullness, the abundance of life that you offer. It is not too late; at least such is our hope. In your mercy hear us, O God, and grant us newness of life, an appreciation of the eternal, and a zeal to share this as extravagantly with others as you have been willing to share it with us. We trust that this can yet be so; we ask it in Jesus' name. Amen.

Words of Assurance
If we are willing to confess our need, God, so full of love and mercy, will forgive us all that brought us to that need, and will so equip us with resources that we experience not need but plenty, not a life that is meager but one that exceeds in abundance all that we can think or imagine. Moreover, not just for us, but for all who so bow before the Almighty; and trusting, pray in his name. Amen.
Praise be to God that we are so raised from poverty to plenty.

Psalter Reading (from Psalm 37)
Trust in the Lord, and do good; so you will live in the land, and enjoy security.
Take delight in the Lord, and he will give you the desires of your heart.
Commit your way to the Lord; trust in him, and he will act.
He will make your vindication shine like the light, and the justice of your cause like the noonday.
Be still before the Lord, and wait patiently for him;
Do not fret over those who prosper in their way, over those who carry out evil devices.

The salvation of the righteous is from the Lord; he is their refuge in time of trouble.
The Lord helps them and rescues them; he rescues them from the wicked and saves them, because they take refuge in him.

Offering Sentences

God's giving is liberal, gracious, available to all, no strings attached. It is never an "ought" with God, but always a willing "glad to." How wonderful when our giving is of the same pattern. It wins friends, strengthens relationships, enables God's work to be done in the world. Let our giving today be of the same spirit.

Prayer of Dedication

Free our lives, O God, for service in your name. Just as we dedicate these monies, the fruits of our labors, so do we consecrate our talents and pledge their use to works of healing, reconciliation, and peacemaking. So would we do our part to advance your kingdom's coming on earth, even as it is known in heaven. Use us to the fullest, O God. Indeed, we are grateful whenever your light can shine through our lives and can so enrich the life of another. So be it. Amen.

Benediction

Trust — in God's way with you. Serve — that God's way be seen in you. Seek to grow — that God's way be perfected in you. And in all and through all, may Christ be your constant companion and guide. So will your life be truly blessed and will you be a blessing to others. Amen!

Blindness/Seeing

Mark 10:46-52
Isaiah 42:14-20

Call to Worship
God sees all — and understands.
We pretend that we see — but misunderstand.
God nonetheless accepts us — and this with a limitless love.
We in worship would dare to accept that love — and so grow in our seeing and understanding.
Thus can our blindness be healed.
Thus can we become fit servants of the Most High.

Invocation
God, you see each one of us as a precious son or daughter. You look within and see the yearning of hearts that would know a way of life that truly satisfies and fulfills. You are aware of the particularity of each of our settings and would minister to us in those settings. You are present to change our blindness to sight, our pretensions to a commitment that truly sees and serves. How amazing that Jesus on his way to Jerusalem was accompanied by sighted disciples who did not see and by a sightless man who did see. Where do we see ourselves in this number? Guide us this day, O God, that whatever our setting, we be led to see — that we might follow Jesus as Savior and Lord and serve him faithfully. Amen.

Call to Confession
There is a blindness, we confess, that masquerades as seeing. We pretend to see — and in the process come to know people in general but never in particular. Thus do friendships elude us; relationships fail to mature. All is but a veneer; we never truly see inside the other, just as we never allow others to see inside us. Are we willing that God change this, and in sighting us that our eyes be opened and our lives be radically remolded into a people seeing in love? Let us so confess our need and our willingness.

Prayer of Confession

God, you have through the years spoken of people who have eyes — and yet see not. Pictured is always a scene of incompleteness, not only of incomprehension and misunderstanding, but of ignorance and poverty. Why is this so? We cannot cast the blame on you, O God, nor can we rightly blame others. That we do not see is in truth due to our own choices — our own *self* interest that in many cases imposes a veil between us and our neighbor. We *choose* not to see — and not only we but others pay the consequences. We rivet our attention on that which we hold to be of value to us, and at the same time fail to discern that of greater value to all, that which defines life itself. Forgive us this blindness, this spiritual blindness. By your mercy sight us, we pray, with vision; vision sensitive to those ways in which we might serve you and all of your creation around us. And most of all, help us to see the face of Christ, for there will we find one worthy of emulation, worthy of the best of heart and mind. It is in his name that we ask it. Amen.

Words of Assurance

The assurance of God is that those of faith shall see and live. Such is the mercy and the omnipotence of God. Here is no fear, but rather a great joy, the throwing off of a mighty burden and the assumption of a glad commitment that with the help of God's love we shall confidently wear.

Praise God for sight — that true vision which means life and hope.

Psalter Reading (from Psalm 34)

I will bless the Lord at all times; his praise shall continually be in my mouth.

My soul makes its boast in the Lord; let the humble hear and be glad.

O magnify the Lord with me, and let us exalt his name together.

I sought the Lord and he answered me, and delivered me from all my fears.

Look to him and be radiant; so your faces shall never be ashamed.
This poor soul cried, and was heard by the Lord, and was saved from every trouble.
The angel of the Lord encamps around those who revere him, and delivers them.
O taste and see that the Lord is good; happy are those who take refuge in him.
The Lord redeems the life of his servants;
None of those who take refuge in him will be condemned.

Offering Sentences
When we see, when we truly see the need of our neighbor, our next step is that of responding. God's love is to flow *through us*. That might well mean our giving of time; it might mean a lending of skills and talents. On other occasions, it will elicit from us an offering of money. So do we come before God now to respond as we can and as need demands — all that God's love be spread to touch and heal and so meet our neighbor's need.

Prayer of Dedication
Help us, O God, to be wise stewards of that entrusted to us. May these gifts now placed upon the table of the Lord be prudently and joyfully used to do the Lord's work. May our eyes ever be open to those opportunities to share of ourselves in your name — that healing and reconciliation take place and that the body of Christ be strengthened. All so that your way may be made fully known on this earth. Amen.

Benediction
May each one of us see — and understand — what God would have us *be* and what God would have us *do* in his name — that we be whole and complete, that our neighbor be blessed in like manner, and that all of creation might indeed rejoice. Amen and amen!

Bread

John 6:24-35
Ephesians 4:7, 11-16

Call to Worship
We come here today to choose.
The choice is between breads: fresh or stale.
It seems that the choice should be an easy one indeed.
We often, however, make it extremely complicated.
The one promotes life; the other gives only an illusion of life.
Though tempting, we must cast aside the illusion, and choose life.
Here is Christ both Strength and Guide.
Let us in word and sacrament rely on him, for his gift is the good bread, indeed the fresh bread, the bread of life.

Invocation
O Christ, Bread of Life, you would break yourself on us, that we be truly fed with that which gives and sustains life. There is no substitute. All else, though promoted with great fanfare and promise, does not endure. Only your mercy, made real by your sacrifice, can cause life to take hold in us — and grow until we too have life, the bread of life, to share with others. So let that happen, right here in our midst, O God, that Christ and Christ's benefits be central to our worship about this table, indeed in all of our living. So be it! Amen!

Call to Confession
Rather than allow ourselves to be fed by Christ, we find ourselves tossed to and fro, blown here and there by many a selfish scheme that strokes our ego, that exalts our way over God's more humble approach to living and giving. Trying to gain center stage, we pursue the illusory rather than the real, and so emerge the loser. Are we willing to confess this, that we might yet find life in Christ?

Prayer of Confession
God, life from your hand is everlastingly fresh and good. It ever has the aroma of newly baked bread. Yet as we look at our lives, we see much that is stale. Our exterior as well as our inner being is too often hard and callous, rather than soft and sensitive and compassionate. Help us to realize the nature of the problem: We fail when we attempt to be the baker, rather than allow you, O God, to be the Author of the bread of life. When we gladly receive from your hand that which truly nourishes, that which you supply in abundance, then will our lives take on a wholesomeness and a texture that will make them a blessing to us and to others. We can then become healthy parts of that one loaf which is the church of Jesus Christ. May that be so in our lives and in the lives of all who look to you for food, for the Bread of Life that fails us not. Amen.

Words of Assurance
Hear these reassuring words of Jesus: "I am the bread of life. Whoever comes to me will never be hungry, and whoever believes in me will never be thirsty ... This is indeed the will of my Father, that all who see the Son of God and believe in him may have eternal life." Such is God's gift to each of us!
Thanks be to God that we shall never hunger. God's bread of life is indeed sufficient!

Psalter Reading (from Psalm 78)
The Lord commanded the skies above, and opened the doors to heaven;
He rained down on them manna to eat, and gave them the grain of heaven.
Mortals ate of the bread of angels; he sent them food in abundance.
He caused the east wind to blow in the heavens, and by his power he led out the south wind;
He rained flesh upon them like dust, winged birds like the sand of the seas;
He let them fall within their camp, all around their dwellings.

And they ate and were filled, for he gave them what they craved. **With upright heart he tended them, and guided them with skillful hand.**

Offering Sentences
Discipleship, our following of Jesus the Christ, calls for us to be vitally concerned with how we share ourselves. How might we give of ourselves in ways that will truly help others? All of us, without exception, have important things to offer, parts of our self that will make a difference in the lives of friend and neighbor and stranger. Let us reflect on this, the gifts that we can offer, as we present for God's use the tithes and the offerings of this day and this worship.

Prayer of Dedication
God, holy, full of wisdom, cause us to listen carefully to your Spirit's prompting as we make decisions regarding the use of these gifts. They represent a part of us, and they are presented gladly that others may be served in your name. May your holy work of spreading the good news here be accomplished, and may many benefit through this sharing, through this act of love reaching out to another. So do we pray, looking to Jesus as the model of that loving, a love forever fresh, a love having the aroma of newly baked bread. Amen.

Benediction
Always let your choice be life. And let that life be refreshed daily by him who is the Bread of Life. The invitation is a simple one indeed: Follow Jesus, and you shall know life, life abundant and eternal. Yea, Lord, may it be so for each one of us!

Challenge

1 Samuel 17:32-46a, 48-50a

Call to Worship
We gather in worship to still our souls.
For we are restless until our souls find their rest in God.
We come here to learn of God's way, a way of life and love and peace.
For we would press upward on that way, until the whole of our lives is joyfully subject to it.
We join here with others to be united as the one family of God.
For we would be prepared for our mission, the challenge of proclaiming good news of membership in God's family to still others.

Invocation
You are the one, O God, who makes things happen, this for our well-being, this for the well-being of all of your creation. Never do you search for an excuse for inaction. Never do you act in ways that are detrimental to communion or community. No task is either so overwhelming or so insignificant that you turn aside and so leave us without guidance, without the wherewithal to take right and decisive action. We ask your presence now, Lord, here during this time of worship, for we need your help, your active participation, so that we may be able to confront and to conquer those giants that threaten to undo us. For there are many; and without the promise of your strength by our side, we fear greatly. Thank you for being here, for this further evidence of your care! May we be attentive to that which you would share with us. Amen.

Call to Confession
Too often we catch ourselves saying, "It can't be done!" before we even try. We listen overmuch to our fears and find ourselves paralyzed by our anxieties. We fail to remember the many times that God has been with us in the past. So do we fail to believe that God will open new ways for us now. Let us rid ourselves of all that

oppresses and depresses, that we be awakened to the strategies and the strength from God that will indeed mean life to us.

Prayer of Confession

Great God and true, you have wonderful and worthwhile things for us to do, things to be done in your name and for the welfare of humankind. We find, however, that giants block our way. These are very real, yet we allow them to immobilize us, this by fear, uncertainty, and indecision. We seemingly forget that you have a part, a crucial part, to play in our battles with giants. You have helped us in the past to survive — and more than survive, to conquer all that would oppress us. Forgive us for not seeing you with us now, providing resources, tools for each new challenge. Strengthen our faith, we pray, that we be assured that trust placed in you is not in vain, but rather wins the day, causing even giants to bow before the majesty of your being and the power of your love. For so will we find a new day dawning for each of us. In the name of Jesus, the one who trusted you completely, do we pray. Amen.

Words of Assurance

Hear these words of Jesus: "My grace is sufficient for you, for my power is made perfect in weakness." Let us rejoice that this grace of God is made available to each of us, that our weakness too might become strength, that the rough places be smoothed, and that the glory of God be revealed through the very story of our salvation.
Thanks be to God that we may live free of fear and are included in God's peaceable kingdom.

Psalter Reading (from Psalm 9)

The Lord is a stronghold for the oppressed, a stronghold in times of trouble.
And those who know your name put their trust in you, for you, O Lord, have not forsaken those who seek you.
Sing praises to the Lord who dwells in Zion. Declare his deeds among the people.

For he who avenges blood is mindful of them; he does not forget the cry of the afflicted.
Be gracious to me, O Lord. See what I suffer from those who hate me; you are the one who lifts me up from the gates of death
So that I may recount all your praises, and, in the gates of daughter Zion, rejoice in your deliverance.

Offering Sentences
The knowledge of God's power available to us brings forth not only words of thanksgiving and praise, but actions born of gratitude, actions that would convey God's love to still others. One such action is that of providing resources for the church's work in the world. We do that through the offering of self that we now consecrate to the Lord's service. Let us present our offering with joy and with the conviction that God indeed works through us.

Prayer of Dedication
Gracious God, guide our giving. Guide it that many may be helped, helped in significant ways that promote healing, understanding, harmony among sisters and brothers. May we never be content with a job half done; rather may we stretch ourselves until our commitment is complete, and we see your kingdom come here on earth. This in Jesus' name. Amen.

Benediction
Giants always meet their match when confronted with God's love. Even those giants that pose the greatest obstacles to life yield before the power of God's redeeming grace. Let us walk then with God, and be hopeful, faithful, trustful of his ways with us. Amen.

Choosing

Joshua 24:1-3a, 14-25
Amos 5:21-24

Call to Worship
We come because God has called us.
Yet it is by conscious decision that we come.
We come because we have been chosen by God.
It remains, though, for us to choose God.
There are many gods that would claim our allegiance.
We come here to worship the one true God, who is Creator, Savior, and Sustainer of all.
Let then our choice be clear — to any who witness who we are and what we do.
Yes, let both our word and our deed proclaim our commitment to the God we serve.

Invocation
God, thank you for giving us a choice. You did not create us that we merely mimic your will. Neither did you create us to be alone, forced to fare for ourselves. Rather, you created us for fellowship, for friendship. True and abiding friendship, we know, demands that choices be made along the way by both parties. It, however, is hindered — it fails — when one party in any way tries to manipulate the other. Thus, again we thank you, holy and gracious God, for giving us the power, the right, to choose, for valuing your relationship with us so highly that we are to enter into it as friend and partner. May we now, having seen you clearly, choose wisely. This, with Christ as our guide. Amen.

Call to Confession
It is not that we don't have the choice. It is that at times we choose poorly. We choose ways of death, when we could have just as well chosen ways of life. We choose ways that, yes, bring temporary pleasure, but disaster in the long term. We find ourselves lured, indeed manipulated, by other gods. Or we choose a god we think

we can control and manipulate. Let us confess the error, the several errors, of our poor choosing, ask forgiveness of the one true God we've ignored, and further implore the nurture and wisdom of that God that we do better in our choosing.

Prayer of Confession
How foolish we are, O God! You offer us the beauty of a relationship with the Holy, one in which we are valued as friend, in which there is freedom to grow, in which there is great and lasting joy. It is a relationship built on love, honor, and respect. Yet we choose to treat it lightly, or ignore it completely, as we turn to other gods, other relationships, ones that play to an obsession deep within that says we must be in control. Forgive us, Lord. May we at long last come to that realization that in choosing your way we in no way diminish self, but rather enhance self, for in so doing we open our lives to all of the many blessings you would share with us. Help us toward that sure belief that by choosing you we are choosing life; and then keep us steady against all that would tempt us and lure us astray. So do we call upon your goodness, your guidance, your eternal presence with us now and always. Amen.

Words of Assurance
The statement is simple and sure: We trust in God's steadfast love. Let us bless God, and remember all that God daily provides: a forgiveness of our sin, a healing of our diseases, the satisfying of us with good, and renewal for all aspects of our living. All is wondrous evidence of God's love and faithfulness.
Praise be to God that even during our moments of turning away, God does not desert us but chooses to love us.

Psalter Reading (from Psalm 119)
Put false ways far from me; and graciously teach me your law.
I have chosen the way of faithfulness; I set your ordinances before me.
I cling to your decrees, O Lord; let me not be put to shame.
I run the way of your commandments, for you enlarge my understanding.

Turn my heart to your decrees, and not to selfish gain.
Turn my eyes from looking at vanities; give me life in your ways.
Confirm to your servant your promise, which is for those who revere you.
See, I have longed for your precepts; in your righteousness give me life.

Offering Sentences
Hear these words of Jesus: "Give, and it will be given to you. A good measure, pressed down, shaken together, running over, will be put in your lap; for the measure you give will be the measure you get back." We have each one of us received of God's abundance. Let us from that abundance bless others and so share the good news of God's love.

Prayer of Dedication
How wonderful it is to know that these offerings, by the guidance of your Spirit, O God, can bring hope to others! How wonderful it is to know that *we* can have a part in your proclamation of good news! Let not only these offerings but our lives be used in this fashion, this day, and during each day of this new week. Amen.

Benediction
The words of Joshua are meant for us too: "Choose this day whom you will serve ... As for me and my house, we will serve the Lord." May you too serve the one true God, Creator, Savior, and Sustainer. Let that be your choice; and may it be apparent in your living. Amen.

Chosen

Isaiah 6:1-8
Luke 5:1-11

Call to Worship
We gather to worship —
That we might scatter to serve.
We are called apart by God —
That equipped we be sent back into the world.
By God's mercy we are chosen —
Chosen not for privilege, but for responsibility.
We are here today to affirm our discipleship —
That our worship be sincere and our service of value.

Invocation
God, you have elected to fashion your good work through human beings, human beings dedicated to your purpose and invested with your power. You choose those without power, yet humble of heart, and make them channels of your love and champions of justice. Though oft times frustrated by the world, they find great joy in your service. So have we been chosen — to serve in your name. Help us this hour to determine with greater clarity what this means; and then equip us, we pray, to carry out our commission, that faithfully we announce the Gospel and live it in the midst of both friend and stranger. All, that your kingdom come on earth as it is in heaven. Amen.

Call to Confession
When God's call comes, we are so apt to misunderstand it. We rightly see it as blessing, but then fail to see the cross, a cross meant for our carrying that comes with it, a cross for each one of us. We identify "chosenness" with privilege. Thus do we miss the mark. Moreover, we shall never see clearly until we confess our ignorance, at times a willful misdirection, and so ready ourselves to receive with our cross God's power to bear it.

Prayer of Confession
We would be true, O God, but there is much to tempt us away from the truth. For truth means an undivided loyalty, an unqualified commitment to love and justice. We would rather compromise — that life might be easy, at least for a time. Truth means faith in you, O God, a total dependence upon you and your way, even though we may not fully understand where the way will lead. We are reluctant to give our whole self; indeed, always it seems we hold back a part of self, and so are prone to a wandering from your way. Truth means knowing the difference between the holy and the profane and a consistent seeking of the holy. We fall short on that one too, O God. Forgive us; challenge us anew. May your call come again, we pray, that with your empowering, this time we follow on the right terms and with the right spirit. Keep before us always the example, the spirit, and the guiding power of Jesus, in whose name we pray. Amen.

Words of Assurance
God is present, here in our midst, to give us yet another chance. We must, however, be ready to receive it, not as a cure-all for the moment but as a radical change in our being and doing, meant for all time. If we are so prepared to heed God's call, it will truly be joy to us and to many another person whose life we shall have the privilege of touching.
Praise be to God that we might yet be servants of the Most High.

Psalter Reading (from Psalm 25)
To you, O Lord, I lift up my soul. O my God, in you I trust.
Make me to know your ways, O Lord; teach me your paths,
Lead me in your truth, and teach me, for you are the God of my salvation; for you I wait all day long.
Be mindful of your mercy, O Lord, and of your steadfast love, for they have been from of old.
Good and upright is the Lord; therefore he instructs sinners in the way.

He leads the humble in what is right, and teaches the humble his way.
All the paths of the Lord are steadfast love and faithfulness, for those who keep his covenant and his decrees.
Who are they that revere the Lord? He will teach them the way that they should choose.

Offering Sentences
God, in calling us, promises to care for us. Thus, we never need to fear want, an emptiness of resources or love or power. We can, therefore, be liberal givers, if all is done with God's will in mind. How generous do we dare be today, as we seek to serve God in love? Let your heart be your guide as you dedicate yourself in this way, through tithes and offerings, to the Lord's work.

Prayer of Dedication
We place our tithes and offerings here before you, O God. Wisdom is now needed that they be expended in a loving and just manner. How many words of hope can they bring, how many acts of mercy, how much upbuilding in love? May your Spirit, O God, work in and through us that satisfactory answers be found to all of these questions — and that in the answering, we discover much joy in serving others in your name. Amen.

Benediction
As it happened in the lives of those first disciples, may we through God's calling find ourselves moving from empty nets to wholesome and full lives. With God this is indeed possible! Will we allow it to happen in us? Let our answer be a resounding "Yes!" May this blessing be upon all!

Connectedness

Luke 24:44-53
Ephesians 1:17-23

Call to Worship
We worship the Christ who promises to be with us always.
Christ has ascended to heaven, there to rule with love and mercy.
Yet God, by taking Christ from us, has not abandoned us.
Christ instead intercedes for us and continues to nurture us.
Indeed, Christ creates the bond that enables us to support one another.
So would we pull each other higher and higher into God's presence.

Invocation
Just like those first disciples, O God, we do not have to worry about our future, for we are assured of your presence with us. We know that by mercy, forgiveness, and love we are connected to you. So can we feel at peace, though the world rage around us. Thanks to you, O God, for this wondrous good news that transforms our whole mode and purpose of living. Moreover, since your love shows no partiality, no one of us can claim to be better or more important than the other. Just as we have together received, so we together reach out to one another and affirm those bonds that make us your church. Indeed, even as we need you, we need one another! So guide us this hour, we pray, by your holy presence that we come to know all the more this connectedness that defines us as family, your family, O God. Amen.

Call to Confession
It is when we doubt God's presence, it is when we begin to feel disconnected, that we begin to complain. We get edgy and irritable with one another. We are hardly of one accord; rather, each tends to go his or her own way. Hurtful criticism is heard, far from God's mandate that we be witnesses of love. Let us confess those

ways in which we spurn Christ's presence, ignore the Spirit that he sends to us, and fail to connect with hope, joy, love, and peace.

Prayer of Confession
Even though Jesus has gone before us to prepare a life-filling and life-fulfilling communion with the Holy, we often fail to display such conviction in our living. Others cannot see how we are connected — connected to the risen Christ — or that we value the acceptance, the love, and the guidance that our Lord provides. So therefore do we lack that depth of fellowship that you, O God, make possible; and the church languishes. We do not grow beyond that point of superficial knowledge one of the other. We do not allow those strong bonds of support to develop that your Spirit would prompt among us. Forgive us, O God. Help us to see what you through the living Christ offer each of us, all of us; and help us to trust you more fully with our lives. For we do wish to be connected with you and with one another, that the way of the healing, reconciling, and uniting Christ be clearly seen here in this congregation of your people. Amen.

Words of Assurance
God has gone up. But God has not gone up and away, leaving us to our confusion. Rather, Christ sits at the right hand of God to intercede for us, to be our Advocate. Moreover, through the gift of the Spirit, we know that we are so connected with the Holy — and with one another. Thus can we be confident about our future and about that work which God would have us do as God's people, the church, here on earth.
Praise be to God! God does not leave us alone. We are connected to the Holy — and through that Spirit to all believers.

Psalter Reading (Psalm 47)
Clap your hands, all you peoples; shout to God with songs of joy.
For the Lord, the most high, is awesome, a great king over all the earth.
He subdued peoples under us, and nations under our feet.
He chose our heritage for us, the pride of Jacob whom he loves.

God has gone up with a shout, the Lord with the sound of a trumpet.
Sing praise to God, sing praises, sing praises to our king, sing praises.
For God is king of all the earth; sing praises with a psalm.
God is king over the nations; God sits on his holy throne.
The princes of the people gather as the people of the God of Abraham.
For the shields of the earth belong to God; he is highly exalted.

Offering Sentences

Even as we are blessed by God's continuing presence, let us find ways to share this blessing with others. This means sharing a portion of ourselves — our time, our talents, our treasure — that others too may feel that they belong, that others may also joyfully see their lives transformed by Christ's reconciling and sanctifying love. So do we now worship God with our tithes and offerings.

Prayer of Dedication

May these gifts of our hearts and hands, O God, fashion strong connections, connections that will link your church to all in the world that is hurting, hoping, hovering on that brink between life and death. Yours, O God, is ever a word of life! May we in all aspects of our living reflect that life in the presence of the risen Christ, with us even as he would be with all peoples everywhere. In his name we pray. Amen.

Benediction

Christ has not abandoned us. Indeed, Christ is with us. Let us then be of a single mind and heart in our service to him and to one another. Let us hold on tenaciously to this lifeline that we have with the Holy. Amen!

Costly Grace

Luke 14:25-35
Philemon 1-21

Call to Worship
God's love is a costly love.
It is costly, yet liberally bestowed.
Indeed, Christ could even forgive those who crucified him.
We too need to learn to walk the second mile — and beyond.
Here in worship we seek to understand and to make our own this higher wisdom of God.
We would do this — by truly hearing the Word and by gathering at the table.

Invocation
Gracious God, your love is longsuffering, for when costly action is required, you do not, you will not, abandon us. You work in our midst that which is needed to love us into submission, knowing that the better course is to win trust rather than compel obedience. In grateful response, we offer you our praise and heart's devotion. We eagerly anticipate your presence during this hour of worship as yet a further demonstration of your care directed to our well-being — as with Word and Spirit you nurture us and so elicit from us an ever greater measure of commitment and joyous participation in your way of life. We do pray in the name of Christ, he who most clearly reflects this love of which we here speak. Amen.

Call to Confession
In our dealings with others, we all too often grow impatient. If we dare to examine our actions carefully, we will discover that there is little about our love that can be called longsuffering. For so it seems, we are more apt to dwell on our "rights" than the other person's needs; and by so doing, not only do we block our own growth in spirit, but thus do the needs of the neighbor go unmet. Lip service to God's way of costly grace is not enough. We are urged to become participants in the drama. Therefore, let us ask

God, yes, that past wrongs be forgiven, but also that wisdom and strength be ours to walk the way of love aright. Let us so pray.

Prayer of Confession
Following faithfully the way of your Son is not easy, O God. Yet with resources that you provide, it is possible. And by so doing, *all* benefit; all find *life*, life that is joyful, full of meaning and purpose. First, you would forgive us, free us from past failings that have built up within us shame and guilt. We humbly ask that you do so, for the burden is heavy indeed. Then we ask of you the gift of compassion, that concern for others that we see in Jesus, for such will equip us for servant living, which can alone build community. Teach us too the cost in so doing, yet grant us, we pray, that joyful resolve to attempt great things for the One who is our Lord and Savior. Thus do we hope to know the basics of being a Christian and so rejoice in the cross of Christ. In the name of your Son do we dare ask these blessings. Amen.

Words of Assurance
Did not Jesus say, "Ask, and it will be given you; search, and you will find; knock, and the door will be opened for you"? So do we ask, search, and knock — that God's way be real to us, and that we find strength of mind, heart, and spirit to follow it faithfully. God's assurance is that of these things, things of worth, we shall not want. **Praise be to God for remaining true to covenant and promise. We shall not want.**

Psalter Reading (from Psalm 86)
Incline your ear, O Lord, and answer me, for I am poor and needy.
Preserve my life, for I am devoted to you; save your servant who trusts in you.
You are my God; be gracious to me, O Lord, for to you do I cry all day long.
Gladden the soul of your servant, for to you, O Lord, I lift up my soul.
For you, O Lord, are good and forgiving, abounding in steadfast love to all who call on you.

Give ear, O Lord, to my prayer; listen to my cry of supplication. In the day of my trouble I call on you, for you will answer me. **There is none like you among the gods, O Lord, nor are there any works like yours.**

Offering Sentences
May we be a people who give in ways that count, who when alert to need seek to address that need whatever the cost, though it demands from us a full measure of understanding, compassion, and grace. For in so doing will we know that we are walking the way of the Christ, and will we find life being lived to the fullest, life abundant and lasting, not only for self but for all. Let us bring forth at this time tithes and offerings which in deed give credence to the good words we speak.

Prayer of Dedication
We need your wisdom, holy God, in routing these gifts — that they initiate healing, bring hope, instill a greater sense of acceptance and belonging in those whose lives they touch. Even as we dedicate this portion of ourselves to your service, may this be but the prelude to a willing gift of all of self, as alert to those ways in which your call will reach us this week, we seek to respond with love, and justice, and peace. Indeed, our greatest blessing is this opportunity that you offer us to serve in your name. So be it! May we act accordingly.

Benediction
It is costly grace, not cheap grace, that defines discipleship. It is from God that we learn this, through the life, death, and resurrection of Jesus Christ, Son of God, our Savior. We shall know this grace in our own lives even as we place the love of Christ first, above all else, and then live that love among all that we meet. This is our calling, a costly calling, but also our joy and our reward. Go forth, and so order your life. In the name of Jesus. Amen!

Dancing With God

2 Samuel 6:1-5, 11-19

Call to Worship
There is joy, joy, joy, joy ...
Yes, deep in our hearts, deep in our hearts ...
Because of what God has done for us;
Because of what God continues to do for us.
Come, and with me dance in the spirit before God.
Let us dance for joy before our Creator and Redeemer.

Invocation
God of exuberance and great gladness, teach us that reverence is not dull and gray, but is light and color, a joyful recounting of blessing. May our worship today reflect cheerful spirits come to pay homage to a Holy Spirit that is bright and beautiful and brimming over with gifts for all who approach. Then through a positive bearing may we communicate this enlivening Word of health, happiness, and hope. For this is indeed the mission that you entrust to us, that we carry forth in Jesus' name. Amen.

Call to Confession
Light, color, joy, a glad recounting of blessing ... Is that a true description of our worship and of who we are as disciples of Jesus Christ? How much dancing before God, dancing *with* God in joyful celebration, have we done lately? If very little, why is that so? Let us look inside ourselves, let us look inside our life as a congregation — that we bring needs, as we see them, before God in prayer.

Prayer of Confession
God, too easily are we weighed down, burdened with many a concern, in truth defeated before we really get started in many of our undertakings. The world throws too much at us, we say, too much that is negative, that ridicules your Gospel, your way of love and peacemaking. And so, little by little, we too turn sour and negative.

All the while, however, you stand by us, hopeful, full of possibilities that when nurtured can bloom into blessings, granting resources that are abundant and apt and able to fulfill. Forgive us this dwelling on the sordid and the incomplete. Help us rather to raise our eyes that we see you near — that we see all of the joy, the liveliness, the purpose, the completeness that you would bring into our lives. You would do that *now*! Why do we wait? Rather let us enjoy at this very moment, this very hour of worship, these glad provisions of your goodness to us. So be it! Amen!

Words of Assurance
God is great; God is good. With Nehemiah of old we can say, "The joy of the Lord is my strength." With David we can say, "Restore to me the joy of thy salvation." Moreover, we hear the words of Jesus, "Enter into the joy of your master." Jesus indeed has opened the way — that all have ready access to the blessing that God affords.
Let us with thanksgiving see life as being full of God's joy; moreover, that God would share that joy with us.

Psalter Reading (from Psalm 98)
O sing to the Lord a new song, for he has done marvelous things.
His right hand and his holy arm have gotten him victory.
Make a joyful noise to the Lord, all the earth;
Break forth into joyous song and sing praises.
Sing praises to the Lord with the lyre, with the lyre and the sound of melody.
With trumpets and the sound of the horn make a joyful noise before the King, the Lord.
Let the sea roar, and all that fills it; the world and those who live in it.
Let the floods clap their hands; let the hills sing together for joy at the presence of the Lord,
For he is coming to judge the earth.
He will judge the world with righteousness, and the peoples with equity.

Offering Sentences
What sort of giver is commended by God? This is clearly stated. It is the cheerful giver. Let us then with joy, with a cheerfulness to what we do, bring forth tithes and offerings — that we might in this manner proclaim God's message of hope, joy, and peace to still others. For many still need to hear this uplifting word, this good news, and take it to heart. Let us so infect them by our giving and by our living.

Prayer of Dedication
Help us, God, to be your good news ambassadors in all of the many settings of our lives. With exuberance, let us reach out to others with your message of hope. Enable us to dance our convictions before both friend and stranger — that they see our faith to be the genuine and wholesome center of our being; moreover, that it is something meant for them too. Use our offerings, we pray, in this manner. We ask it in Jesus' name. Amen.

Benediction
There is joy, joy deep in our hearts, because of God's continuing goodness to us all. As we dance before the Lord, may others see and be glad and join the dance — that each one of us learn how to celebrate life to the fullest. Amen.

Deafness/Hearing

Mark 7:31-37
Isaiah 35:4-7a

Call to Worship
Let us open our eyes —
To the wonder of God's goodness, God's love that fills this universe.
Let us open our ears —
To the wisdom of God's Word, the guidance it offers to life's journey.
Let us open our mouths —
To sound forth praise, the good news of redemption and release.
So let our worship be a full participation of self.
So let this company of God's people rejoice.

Invocation
Yours is a wondrous ability, O God, to open eyes and unstop ears. Those who heretofore have failed to see your glory can now rejoice in your way that leads with love. Those who have been deaf to your Word can now feel its redeeming and reconciling impact on their lives. So would you open *us*, unstop *us*, to the joy of living. Let that happen this hour, we pray, as we listen to your Word and as we allow ourselves to be led by your Spirit, thus preparing self for service in your name. Make us ever a glad people, thankful for the life you bestow, ready to celebrate it and use it to the fullest. In Jesus' name. Amen.

Call to Confession
As we open eyes and ears to life about us, let us be aware of God at work in many a situation of need close at hand. For God might well desire to co-opt us — that we labor with the Almighty to bring health and wholeness of life to those we'd otherwise overlook. Indeed, overlooking a sister or brother in need is cause for confession.

Prayer of Confession
Oft times, O God, our sins of omission are more grievous, more difficult to explain, than those mistakes we make openly and atone for. To be ignorant of need, need right before us, is most assuredly a betrayal of your way of life. To be deaf to another's plea for help fails utterly to reflect the caring that Christ's love asks, yea demands, of us. It finally becomes apparent even to us that we cannot use as an excuse our blindness or our deafness — or our busyness. Yet how insulated we remain from the needs of others. If we would but look to you, Lord, our eyes would be opened, our ears unstopped, our body, mind, and spirit charged into action. Even as you are forgiving of past errors, help us to be fully awake and aware that we might serve you faithfully in the present. Hold before us that need which we might otherwise overlook, and show us how we can indeed make a difference. This, in Christ's name. Amen.

Words of Assurance
"Once you were darkness, but now in the Lord you are light. Live as children of light, for the fruit of the light is found in all that is good and right and true." So does God in Christ enable us to be and do. So do we bring into being a caring community. Thus is there reconciliation and healing — and finally a whole people who live together in peace.
Glory and thanksgiving to Christ who makes this possible, who opens to us a new way of living, one that both challenges and fulfils.

Psalter Reading (from Psalm 66)
Come and see what God has done; he is awesome in his deeds among mortals.
He turned the sea into dry land; they passed through the river on foot.
There we rejoiced in him who rules by his might forever, whose eyes keep watch on the nations — let the rebellious not exalt themselves.
Bless our God, O peoples, let the sound of his praise be heard,

Who has kept us among the living, and has not let our feet slip.
For you, O God, have tested us; you have tried us as silver is tried.
You brought us into the net; you laid burdens on our back; you let people ride over our heads;
We went through fire and through water; yet you have brought us out to a spacious place ...
Come and hear, all you who revere God,
And I will tell you what he has done for me.

Offering Sentences
If once we were deaf and could now hear, hear even the faintest of sounds, what pray tell would be our response? Would it not be wonderment, jubilation, and thanksgiving? If once we were totally blind and suddenly could see, see everything clearly, how pray tell would we act? Would it not be with amazement, great joy, and an elation that immediately turns to gratitude? If *we* because of Christ can now hear and see, what shall be *our* response? A glad offering, a jubilant offering of self that seeks to thank and to serve the Author of these gifts of life, life made new. Let us now bring forth that offering.

Prayer of Dedication
God of great abundance, how pleased you are when we take fullness of life and share it with another. For there is always enough to go around. In this way is our joy complete — in the serving of gifts of life to those in need. May these offerings be used to that end — so that all may benefit, so that all may have enough. For this indeed *is* the way of the Christ. Amen.

Benediction
Go forth into the world and, with ears unstopped, listen for that particular call to service that God will send your way this week. And then with great energy and zeal pursue it — with the best that you can offer. God, you will find, will then gladly supply the rest.

Depth Of Devotion

Mark 7:1-9, 14-15, 21-23
James 1:22-27

Call to Worship
We are not here for show.
We are here to express a depth of devotion.
We are here that the inner being be renewed.
We are here that hearts be guided in ways of righteousness and peace.
All of this as a fit and pleasing worship of God —
That on hearing the word, we be led to do it.

Invocation
God, we like to be thought of as religious. We have our rituals and our traditions. We follow that format which each Sunday would tell others around us that we are a faithful people. Yet it is not ritual, tradition, or form that ensures a true worship. We need to approach you with a willing heart, an open mind, and an humble spirit. Our motives must be pure, our desires focused upon your will for our lives. May this indeed be evident in our worship today — that we leave here a people refreshed and ready to serve. You, Lord, are here to share with us from the abundance of your love. May we, in turn, assume that posture which will enable us to enter into communion with you. This, in Jesus' name. Amen.

Call to Confession
How much of our worship is veneer — attractive on the outside, but of lesser substance and value within? How much is merely superficial, making us for the moment feel good, yet having no depth, no enduring worth? Dare we take a hard look at our worship and what we bring to it, that we ask in all honesty how fit an offering it is to the God who meets us here in this place? Let us focus on this as we unite in words of confession.

Prayer of Confession
Lord God, we confess that we invest far too little time in cultivating a close relationship with you. It's like so much of life today — many acquaintances, but few true friends. You invite us into the fullness of a communion that is blessing beyond measure. Yet we are content with skimming the surface, doing what custom and propriety demand, but no more. We may indeed be here to worship, yet how much of a day, every day, do we devote to seeking, serving, and then resting in your presence? Truly, we have much growing yet to do in our understanding of what constitutes a joyful and full existence. Help us, we pray! How we rejoice that you are always near, faithful to us, your creation, and so would lead us in life's way. It is so very much more than we deserve, but then again your grace is indeed amazing. Do your work in us, O God. Amen.

Words of Assurance
God in Christ indeed is present and would dwell in our hearts through faith. So are we rooted and grounded in love — and can begin to comprehend with the saints what is the breadth and length and height and depth of divine love. So are we filled with the fullness of God.
Thanks be to God for life that is renewed, strengthened, and given purpose.

Psalter Reading (Psalm 15)
O Lord, who may abide in your tent? Who may dwell on your holy hill?
Those who walk blamelessly, and do what is right, and speak the truth from their heart;
Who do not slander with their tongue, and do no evil to their friends,
Nor take up a reproach against their neighbors;
In whose eyes the wicked are despised, but who honor those who revere the Lord;
Who stand by their oath even to their hurt;
Who do not lend money at interest, and do not take a bribe against the innocent.
Those who do these things shall never be moved.

Offering Sentences
Our gifts are not to impress, but rather are offered to instill hope in others, who by this means discover that God cares and that God's children care. May divine love, the *agape* of God, be found in all that we do, that as doers of the Word we utilize to the fullest those talents bestowed on us by the Almighty. Thus will our worship be complete.

Prayer of Dedication
O God, may others be truly gifted by what we have done here today, by that which we here offer in your name. For our giving serves but a single purpose: that your name be glorified. Moreover, you have shown us that this can be done best by serving the neighbor in need. Help us to accept each challenge that comes our way, each invitation, each opportunity to serve — that we meet each with love, patience, understanding, indeed all of the resources that we can muster. May it be so with these offerings and all others of the week ahead. Amen.

Benediction
Let ours be a faith deep-seated in the heart, one that reaches out to those in need, one evident in our every action. So will it be real — and not sham. So will *we* be real, the children of God we are meant to be. May it be so with you, for then shall you know true joy and purpose in your living. Go forth in this manner to love and to serve. Amen.

Dwelling Place

2 Samuel 7:1-14, 17

Call to Worship
Though we call this God's house, we know that God does not dwell in a house made by human hands.
Indeed, God is spirit, and we come to worship in spirit and in truth.
God is present wherever we may be; God's love, God's power is ever near.
It remains for us to recognize this and to welcome God into every setting of our lives, including this time of gathering for praise and thanksgiving, for learning and dedication anew.
For even as we ask, "Where does God live?" we would answer, "God lives in us."
We are God's temple, the spirit of God dwelling in us.
Let our worship now reflect this wondrous affirmation.
Let our living for God reflect the same glorious fact day by day.

Invocation
God, you are a God on the move. It is not your habit to sit still, to dwell in one place, to invest yourself in a particular time. We thank you for that, for thus can you be near to us; thus can you be active in this present moment. Moreover, how awesome and how humbling is this desire of yours to live in us, that your will be expressed in our being and in our actions. That calls for a personal commitment on our part. So do we come to learn what you expect of us — that we then might make our pledge of loyalty and faithfulness. Therefore, visit us today, we pray, with the wonder of your being and lead us into a commitment that is joyous and complete. Amen.

Call to Confession
Though we like God to be available when out of need we call upon the Almighty, we nonetheless would rather not have God

looking over our shoulder all the time. For at times we cherish our privacy. We'd rather that God stay in his house and we in ours. Yet how quick we are to criticize and to say, "How long, O Lord?" when God appears to be absent and there is no holy intervention. Let us confess this ambivalence we have to God's being with us.

Prayer of Confession

God, do we not know that you are with us wherever we go? Rather than cause us alarm, this knowledge should bring us assurance. All of your resources — mighty in power, compassionate in application — are available for our well-being. Can we not see that by your actions you heal, and that you would use us — as your house and as your people — to carry the same good news to others? The only house you care to dwell in, O God, is a faithful people. Forgive us when by our reluctance and our inattentiveness we have spurned this, your holy will. Instill in us, we pray, the desire to represent you fully and faithfully by our every word and deed. This is our plea. In your mercy, hear us and heal us. In Jesus' name. Amen.

Words of Assurance

Hear anew those words of wisdom of old: "Unless the Lord builds the house, those who would build it labor in vain. Unless the Lord guards the city, those who guard it watch in vain." Praise be to God — that God both builds and guards, that we might be whole and our community holy — this through Jesus Christ, who is the Lord. **Praise God — for wherever God is, there is home.**

Psalter Reading (from Psalm 84)

How lovely is your dwelling place, O Lord of hosts!
My soul longs, indeed it faints for the courts of the Lord; my heart and my flesh sing for joy to the living God.
Even the sparrow finds a home, and the swallow a nest for herself, where she may lay her young, at your altars, O Lord of hosts, my King and my God.
Happy are those who live in your house, ever singing your praise.

Happy are those whose strength is in you ... they go from strength to strength.
O Lord God of hosts, hear our prayer; give ear, O God of Jacob! Behold our shield, O God; look on the face of your anointed.
For a day in your courts is better than a thousand elsewhere.
I would rather be a doorkeeper in the house of my God than live in the tents of wickedness.
For the Lord God is a sun and shield; he bestows favor and honor. No good thing does the Lord withhold from those who walk uprightly.
O Lord of hosts, happy is everyone who trusts in you.

Offering Sentences
God is present — to meet our every need. God calls for us also to be present, sharing that which God has given us to meet the neighbor's need, so making available the largesse of God, God's love, that through this sharing there be scarcity for none. So do we bring our tithes and offerings, giving new meaning to "gifts of God for the people of God."

Prayer of Dedication
You place great significance, Lord, on our giving, for it is your way of reaching out beyond this place to touch with healing those in need of health and hope, those who desperately desire renewal of purpose and spirit. So may these tithes and offerings be an extension of your holy love, your care for all of creation. Thus will they be seen as part of that total giving we have come to know in Christ, for it is in his name that we ask this. Amen.

Benediction
Go from this place convinced that you are God's temple, that God's spirit indeed dwells in you. What an awesome affirmation! What wondrous possibilities! What a great responsibility! Just remember that God is always present to aid and to guide; moreover, that God's resources are abundantly available — that we are to share even as God shares. Amen.

Easter

Matthew 28:1-10
Romans 6:3-11

Call to Worship
We come to share and to shout good news.
Christ lives and so shall we!
Darkness has yielded to the light of a new day.
We stand in that light, dumbfounded yet with great joy.
For the gift of eternal life hangs in the balance;
And God has tipped that balance in our favor.
Alleluia! God's love is expressed in life!
Death no more shall reign — in us or in any child of God!

Invocation
Amid the beauty of an Easter morn, we come to this place of worship to make known our praise and our thanksgiving. For you, Lord God, stand before us as both Author of life and Restorer of life. So great is your love for us that when we horribly botch your gift of life, you are nonetheless present to forgive and to gift us again. This we see clearly in the life, death, and resurrection of your Son Jesus. By means of his resurrection, we know that death cannot exercise dominion over us. We are freed to live a meaningful and purposeful life, a life of great joy and communion with you and with sisters and brothers united in your love. Our hearts thus overflow with gladness and with gratitude. May our witness to this new life be apparent to all — this day and every day. In the name of the Risen Christ do we offer this, our prayer. Amen.

An Easter Litany
The messengers of this new day run to tell us:
Christ is risen! Christ is risen indeed!
The tomb is empty; our hearts are full.
So has God gifted us with holy love.
Our mourning has been turned to dancing; our tears, to laughter.
Christ is risen! How glorious! Christ is risen indeed!

No longer captive to any lesser power, the prisoner has been set free.
So has God gifted us with holy love.
Death clothes are cast aside. Greetings of life bind up broken hearts.
Christ is risen! Christ is risen indeed! His words are for us.
The lowly are so lifted; the pretentious, brought low.
Such is the power and the working of holy love.
Thus is the promise of God fulfilled in our presence.
For we can see that Christ is risen! He is risen indeed.
So would we too be messengers to share the good news, wherever we go, in word and deed.
For we have holy love to share — and life. Alleluia! Alleluia!

Psalter Reading (from Psalm 98)
O sing to the Lord a new song, for he has done marvelous things.
His right hand and his holy arm have gotten him victory.
The Lord has made known his victory;
He has revealed his vindication in the sight of the nations.
He has remembered his steadfast love and faithfulness to the house of Israel.
All the ends of the earth have seen the victory of our God.
Make a joyful noise to the Lord, all the earth;
Break forth into joyous song and sing praises.
Sing praises to the Lord with the lyre, with the lyre and the sound of melody.
With trumpets and the sound of the horn make a joyful noise before the King, the Lord.

Offering Sentences
Joy and thanksgiving abound on this Resurrection morn. We express that from the heart in many a glad way. Our tithes and offerings too are a cheerful response to love and life and new beginnings. For they can be used to share the good news; they can bring God's love in very practical ways to persons in need of healing; they can awaken new life in the spirit. Let us so share our Easter joy!

Prayer of Dedication
Easter is not only a day. It is a verb. May these expressions of thanksgiving, O God, these offerings, through the presence of your love and Spirit, easter new beginnings in lives now burdened with doubt, disappointment, yes even despair. Such is the power of resurrection and new life that you share with us this day, and always. May we and the gifts we provide be channels through which this power can act — in life-changing and life-enhancing ways — this that the love of the Risen Christ be known to many others. Amen.

Benediction
The day is still young. Good news is to be shared. Let us go forth as renewed, enthusiastic children of God — to extend the reach of the long arm of God's love in many a helpful and needful way. All, in the name of the Risen Christ. Amen!

Father

Ephesians 6:1-4

Call to Worship
There is a vastness and wonder to God that we can in no way describe.
Yet there is a closeness and intimacy to God that we call Father.
Our worship is thus filled with awe, with words about God that are woefully inadequate.
Yet there is certainty and tenderness in one word: Father.
Let our worship then reflect both the grandeur and the personal nature of the one God.
Let us give thanks to the great God of the Universe, who nonetheless comes to us and cares for us as a heavenly Parent.

Invocation
We are here, O God, to learn what it means to live as family, with you as the Parent and we as children. Family, you would teach us, is to be closely-knit, each member a valued part of the whole, yet with one clearly the head, on whom all others depend for guidance, for encouragement, and for drawing all together in unity. Gladly do we acknowledge you to be the head. Willingly do we depend upon the way in which you would lead us. Teach us yet further lessons today, we pray, lessons that will enable us to strengthen the ties of family, lessons that will assist in bringing all into accord with your holy Word and Spirit. Such is our prayer as we begin this hour of worship. So be it. Amen.

Call to Confession
In many a willful way do we introduce disharmony within the human family, and so do we fail to follow faithfully God's call that we be members united to one another in loyalty to a heavenly family. We pull this way and that in order that our own ambition might rule, rather than comply with the more humble task of being a servant member of the whole body. Let us confess unto God our

restlessness, our willingness to be tempted, and the very personal need for forgiveness that follows.

Prayer of Confession

Patient and loving Father, how many times you have shown us the way, only to have us spurn the resources for abundant living that you offer. We would rather follow our separate yearnings — which are shallow and selfish. How we must grieve you, as did that prodigal son of old. Yet like that compassionate and faithful father, you long for our return and are prepared joyously to welcome us again into the family. It falls to us that with repentant hearts we acknowledge our need and recognize your goodness. We use this very moment in our lives to do that. We confess the various ways we have separated ourselves from the wellspring of life and love that flows from your being, and we ask to be received home. Father, may we once again be called your children. Indeed, help us to act like children of the Most High. We look to your Son Jesus to show us how. Amen.

Words of Assurance

"The Lord is merciful and gracious, slow to anger and abounding in steadfast love ... He does not deal with us according to our sins, nor repay us according to our iniquities. For as the heavens are high above the earth, so great is his steadfast love toward those who revere him; as far as the east is from the west, so far does he remove our transgressions from us. As a father has compassion for his children, so the Lord has compassion for those who revere him."

Thanks be to God for such patience, for such concern, for mercy, and for the power to forgive.

Psalter Reading (from Psalm 89)

You said, "I have made a covenant with my chosen one, I have sworn to my servant David:
'I will establish your descendants forever, and I will build your throne for all generations.'"

My faithfulness and steadfast love shall be with him; and in my name his horn shall be exalted.
I will set his hand on the sea and his right hand on the rivers.
He shall cry to me, "You are my Father, my God, and the Rock of my salvation!"
I will make him the firstborn, the highest of the kings of the earth.
For I will keep my steadfast love for him, and my covenant with him shall stand firm.
Blessed be the Lord forever. Amen and amen.

Offering Sentences
What father would give his son or daughter a serpent? If we would give only good gifts to our children, how much more will our Father in heaven give good gifts to us, his children! And now, in thanksgiving, what will we return to the Father as gift? Let us worship God with our tithes and offerings, our response of gratitude, this that God's gracious will and his mighty works might be known by still others, those who need to hear and see and so live.

Prayer of Dedication
In God's economy, no gift is wasted. Thus, we know that these gifts, O God, can be and will be routed by you to places of need — there to awaken hearts, to heal bodies, to rouse spirits, and to bring people into community. Your love can do this! Therefore, we entrust these gifts to the leading of your love. And noting the results, may we be willing to give more and more — that your name be praised and your will be done, here and everywhere. Amen.

Benediction
May those who are parents ever be guided by God the Father. May we all find our lives indelibly marked by the mercy, the persistence, the never-failing care of that Holy Parent, the Father, who claims us, yes indeed, every one of us. Amen!

Forgiveness

Matthew 18:21-35

Call to Worship
O God, we enter your gates with thanksgiving;
And your courts with praise.
Your steadfast love endures forever;
And your faithfulness to all generations.
Your forgiveness has been present on so many occasions.
More than seven times seven times seven.
How can we respond but with joy as forgiveness washes us clean?
Gladness floods our hearts; so are we led anew in your way.
Thus, Lord, receive our worship.
We lift voice and heart; we offer praise and thanksgiving.

Invocation
God, full of grace and mercy, you offer forgiveness to all your children. However, we who receive it often refuse to extend the same to others. Give us, we pray, generous spirits, that we not heap up conditions upon the forgiveness we offer, but that we be able to forgive even those who will not forgive in return. In doing so, let us imitate Jesus, who had compassion for all, including the very ones who nailed him to the cross. It is in his name that we begin our worship; it is in his name that we pray. Amen.

Call to Confession
We too often keep score rather than maintain a ledger of grace. We proclaim an eye for an eye and a tooth for a tooth, rather than rejoice in a forgiveness that brings reconciliation and new life. Let us acknowledge our need to grow in this very crucial aspect of our faith and our life together.

Prayer of Confession
Merciful God, Jesus spoke of us saying, "Father, forgive them"; but we have said of others, "They do not deserve our forgiveness."
Lord, have mercy upon us.

Jesus spoke of us saying, "Father, forgive them"; but we have said of others, "We can *never* forgive them; just look at what they have done."
Christ, have mercy upon us.
Jesus spoke of us saying, "Father, forgive them"; but we have said of others, "No way! Too many times have we been hurt by them."
Christ, have mercy upon us.
Jesus spoke of us saying, "Father, forgive them"; but we have said of others, "Justice demands punishment. Only then will we think of mercy."
Lord, have mercy upon us.
Merciful God, Jesus taught us to pray, "Forgive us our sins, as we forgive those who sin against us."
Forgive us, Lord, when at times we display very unforgiving hearts. Let your ever-present forgiveness cause us to remove from our minds and from our living the lists of grievances we keep. May your readiness to forgive correct our vision which can be so shortsighted, that we can sense the joy and peace that comes from the word of forgiveness we offer. It is in knowing how much you have forgiven that moves us to be forgiving too. This, in Jesus' name. Amen.

Words of Assurance
Jesus' words to the repentant thief on the cross, "Today you will be with me in Paradise," are his words to us as well. How can we receive these utterly amazing words without their influencing our whole attitude on life and everything around? Let us acknowledge our own forgiveness with a life of forgiveness, a life lived for others in Jesus' name.
Blessing and honor, glory and power be unto the God of grace and mercy.

Psalter Reading (from Psalm 103)
The Lord is merciful and gracious, slow to anger and abounding in steadfast love.
He will not always accuse, nor will he keep his anger forever.

He does not deal with us according to our sins, nor repay us according to our iniquities.
For as the heavens are high above the earth, so great is his steadfast love toward those who revere him;
As far as the east is from the west, so far he removes our transgressions from us.
As a father has compassion for his children, so the Lord has compassion for those who revere him.

Offering Sentences

As followers of the Christ, we are to confirm words of mercy with deeds of mercy. Allow your discipleship to lead you into distinct paths of service, responding to need whenever and wherever you encounter that need in your daily walk. Let us give evidence of this willingness as we bring forward this day's tithes and offerings — for the work of Christ's church in this place.

Prayer of Dedication

Do we even have an inkling of the joy that these gifts will bring into the lives of others, the many ways in which they will cross boundaries to bring people together in Christ, the pain that they will help to alleviate, the new beginnings and the new life that they will prompt? God, you know the good that can issue forth from these gifts. By your Spirit direct them — and us — to those places where what is here offered can best serve your kingdom's coming on earth, as it is in heaven. Lead us forward, O God, into your future. Amen.

Benediction

Each time during this new week that you are tempted to keep score, turn rather to God's provision of grace. Draw from it, as much as you like, as much as you need, to create for yourself and for others around you a forgiven and forgiving community, one willing to allow Christ's peace to enter and to reign. Amen!

Freedom

James 1:25
Romans 13:8-14a

Call to Worship
We praise the God who made us —
For so are we created that we might freely enter into communion with God.
We praise God for community —
A community ordained by God where love, freedom, and justice reign.
We praise God for this time of worship —
An hour when we together might grow in spirit, where through heart, mind, and soul all in freedom can approach God.

Invocation
We place a high value indeed, O God, upon that freedom which allows us individually and as a community to be your children, this in the midst of a world that still seeks freedom's true meaning. We find that we grow as we use this freedom responsibly — to develop particular talents, but then to share them for the well-being of all. Just as we strive toward our own potential, so would you have us, in freedom, jealously guard the rights of others. We depend on your nurturing in worship, O God — that we understand all of this aright and that with insight and determination we seek those ways in which we can be doers of your holy will. So lead us this hour, we pray, that the responsible use of freedom truly be the centerpiece of all that we do together. This in Christ's name. Amen.

A Litany of Freedom and Peace
It was so from the beginning of the story and has been at all times since:
You created us human beings, O God, to be free.
The trek under Moses out of Egypt was a pilgrimage to freedom.
All because, O God, you have created us to be free.

Jesus came that we might know the truth, for the truth would set us free.

All because, O God, as redeemed children you would have us enjoy the fruits of freedom.

Saints through the centuries have urged a responsible use of freedom.

All because, O God, in our enjoyment of freedom you would not have us withhold this freedom from another.

We would that ours be a nation of peace.

This, we know, can come to pass only as all in the land are free.

We would that ours be a world at peace.

This, we know, can come to pass only as each nation respects the freedom of all other nations.

We are thankful for all who in advocating freedom become peacemakers.

They receive your gift of peace, O God, and seek to bestow it freely not upon some but upon all.

Praise be your holy way, O God, that leads from freedom to peace.

May we, your people, seek to follow it faithfully, both now and forever. Amen.

Offering Sentences

Our giving to God, designed for the well-being of others, is also an expression of our freedom. For we are not constrained in any way in our giving. We are not compelled to give any certain amount. Our giving need not be channeled in any particular way. In truth, we have freedom to respond in whatever way our heart and mind shall dictate. Let us then, as we worship, thank God for this freedom; and through the tithes and the offerings that we bring, speak in a convincing and freeing way to others at their point of need.

Prayer of Dedication

Gracious God, assist us, we pray, in the directing of these gifts — to places that others might neglect, that they give encouragement and a sense of acceptance to those who would otherwise be left out. In a free land, help us to use our freedom responsibly, alert to the neighbor that needs a helping hand. Nothing holds us back; we can even now reach others with the love of Christ. It is in his name that we pray. Amen.

Benediction
As we depart this place to serve God in the world, we remember anew the cost that others have paid for freedom, freedom that we now enjoy — and in doing so, let us be thankful. Also, let us note and not forget those who still need to taste freedom in all its fullness; and let us dedicate ourselves to those tasks, those freeing tasks, that are still to be done, in every instance relying on the prompting and the power of the Holy Spirit. Go in peace; so serve your neighbor in the name of and with the love of Jesus Christ our Lord. Amen!

Friend

John 15:9-17

Call to Worship
We come to worship the Christ, who though he was in the form of God became servant of all.
We would be a servant church that follows faithfully a servant Lord.
We marvel that Christ calls us to be ambassadors of reconciliation, such a wondrous and responsible calling.
So would we humbly but resolutely become partners in Christ's work of making people and creation whole.
In a most intimate moment Christ bestowed upon his disciples the name friend.
So would we count such a name our greatest honor.

Invocation
You treat us, Lord, in such a high and honored way. You who are all-wise, all-powerful, and all-loving nonetheless bestow upon us, such a small part of your creation, great responsibility and a position of worth in your presence. You call us friend, and you would have us be your agents of reconciliation, in this manner carrying forth your work on this earth. How can we possibly be up to the task? It can be so, you tell us, even as we keep your commandment that we love one another as you love us. Help us in our worship today to understand better what that means. For, Lord, we would be true; we would be faithful. We would have our fruit be good fruit and have joy surround our every endeavor. All in your name, O Lord, that your will be done. Amen.

Call to Confession
It takes work to cultivate a friendship. One cannot assume that it will happen. A nurturing is required, a nurturing that is ongoing, for friendship is never static but is continually evolving. At times we fail to see this work as essential — and our friendships suffer, even our friendship with Christ. Are we willing to admit this, to

confess our need, and so ask forgiveness, direction, and power for our future?

Prayer of Confession
O living Christ, you would relate to us, to each one of us, in a very intimate and lasting way. You call us friends. It was you who took the initiative and sought the relationship. It's more than we could ever have expected — or hoped for. Just imagine: We are partners with the Christ of God in a common service! What an honor! And yet, how often we have shunned the gracious invitation to work together. How often we have failed to join you at your table, or devote ourselves to the hard work of proclaiming your gospel in a broken world. We have failed to value and to cause this friendship to mature; and then we wonder why it is not any more significant. Forgive us, we pray; open our eyes to your presence with us even now and show us those very practical steps we can take to make real and pleasing our friendship with you, even as we serve the needs of our neighbor. We ask this, trusting in your mercy and in your continuing desire to hold us close. Amen.

Words of Assurance
Praise you, God, for you are patient and kind. Though we disappoint you, yet you are however willing to forgive and to remember our broken past no more. You guide us into a new day, this by the love of Christ and by the cleansing and renewing power of your Holy Spirit.
Thanks be to God! We *are* forgiven! Jesus calls us friend and directs us anew.

Psalter Reading (from Psalm 95)
O come, let us sing to the Lord;
Let us make a joyful noise to the rock of our salvation!
Let us come into his presence with thanksgiving;
Let us make a joyful noise to him with songs of praise!
For the Lord is a great God, and a great King above all gods.
In his hands are the depths of the earth; the heights of the mountains are his also.

The sea is his, for he made it,
And the dry land, which his hands have formed.
O come, let us worship and bow down; let us kneel before the Lord, our Maker!
For he is our God, and we are the people of his pasture, and the sheep of his hand.

Offering Sentences

"Love one another as I have loved you." Those words of Jesus establish the parameters of our sharing with one another. May they ever guide us in our giving, as we allow heart, mind, and spirit to dwell upon them and to translate intention into deed. So do we worship and proclaim our loyalty to Christ in the giving of tithes and offerings.

Prayer of Dedication

Guiding and empowering God, avenues for service are ever opening before us. Help us to see them and devote ourselves to them with enthusiasm and zeal. What we give, when offered to others in the presence of your love, is multiplied in wondrous and amazing ways. May we be witness to that many times over during the week ahead — that your kingdom come and your will be done *on earth* as it is in heaven. Amen.

Benediction

Depart from here carrying proudly the name "Friend of Christ." Do your part, and work to cultivate this friendship, for most assuredly Jesus will do his part. And see where that will lead you, as you seek to grow in your faith and in service to God and neighbor. Amen.

Garments

Ephesians 4:25—5:2
John 6:35, 41-51

Call to Worship
We come to be clothed as children of God.
Indeed, we would put on the spirit of Christ.
This is truly a garment like no other.
How can we possibly learn to wear it?
Jesus himself gives the answer and shows us the way.
Let us then as we worship allow him full rein.

Invocation
God, you offer us that which is full and lasting — that which measures to the fullness of Christ, that which endures for all time even unto eternity. Life in your care and with your leading thus has meaning and purpose and presents each day as an exciting opportunity for growth and service. So do we come in worship to express our thanksgiving and to take on the challenge of your call. We look for your holy presence among us and wait attentively for that which you would share with us this hour. All, in Jesus' name and to proclaim his glory. Amen.

Call to Confession
We love to clothe ourselves in garments of our own making, purchased on credit, that we imagine will be paid for with the sweat of our hands and brow. These garments are often costly and lavish, well beyond our means, not linked well at all to the essentials of living. These decisions to acquire on many occasions lead us to bankruptcy. And then, pray tell, to whom can we turn? God invites us to turn to the Holy, to the true Provider, and there with humble and contrite heart to find life, life in abundance.

Prayer of Confession
God of mercy, God of purpose and accomplishment, we have good intentions, but how frequently we find ourselves traveling down

side roads of our own making. Soon we are far from the center of being, far from the embrace of your caring and guiding love. We dress ourselves in garments that soon wear out, that identify us in ways detrimental to growth and joy. We want more out of life, but claim that we know not where to turn. Help us to recall, O God, that your invitation is still very much there — that we turn to you, not only to find relief from a past that is now burden, but to be marked by hope for life still to be received as gift. Here in your presence we find both a forgiveness and a direction. Thank you, God, for remaining near, for not abandoning us to our own desires and devices. We do now turn to you and ask that we might truly live the blessing of your mercy and power and love. In Jesus do we know this to be possible. Amen.

Words of Assurance
Hear these words of assurance, words of the Apostle Paul: "If anyone is in Christ, there one finds a new creation. Everything old has passed away; see, all has become new! All of this is from God, who reconciled us to himself in Christ ... For our sake, he made him to be sin who knew no sin, so that in him we might become the righteousness of God."
Praise God for dressing us in that garment which truly spells life for us — one that fits, that fulfills, one that is forever.

Psalter Reading (Psalm 130)
Out of the depths I cry to you, O Lord. Lord, hear my voice!
Lord, hear my voice! Let your ears be attentive to the voice of my supplications!
If you, O Lord, should mark iniquities, Lord, who could stand?
But there is forgiveness with you, so that you may be revered.
I wait for the Lord, my soul waits, and in his word I hope;
My soul waits for the Lord more than those who watch for the morning; more than those who watch for the morning.
O Israel, hope in the Lord! For with the Lord there is steadfast love, and with him is great power to redeem.
It is he who will redeem Israel from all its iniquities.

Offering Sentences
What *is* an appropriate gift to the God who loves us? Can it be anything less than a life devoted in service to his name? Let us give from a depth of heart's devotion and from a conviction that daily finds its purpose renewed. Let us give all within our ability to give, gladly, and with the good of others in mind.

Prayer of Dedication
We depend upon your wisdom, O God; we depend upon your wisdom to direct us in the use of these gifts that we here present to your church. Move these offerings with a right spirit into those arenas of service where life-giving, life-enhancing words and acts are needed. May our witness thus be a true sign of your love. Amen.

Benediction
May all of us wear humbly those garments of life and love that show us to be children of God. May others, as they see us wear these garments faithfully, also turn to God — and so accept the abundance of good gifts that the Holy and Almighty One offers. Amen.

Giving/Greed

Mark 12:41-44
Matthew 27:3-10

Call to Worship
We worship the one God, Creator and Sustainer of all:
The God of the sanctuary, as well as the God of the market place.
We worship the one God, who rules both time and eternity:
The Lord of the Sabbath, as well as the Lord of every day's journey.
We worship the one God, who touches every aspect of life:
A God concerned about the whole person and the whole community.
We worship the one God, God of the universe and God of our human family:
Infinite, yet as close and as personal as a loving parent.

Invocation
Gracious, all-wise and all-providing God, your focus is always on those things of worth that money cannot buy. There is a host of such things, and together they make up the abundant life, your promise to us. We can name peace and love and hope and friendship and joy, to mention just a few. All of these are gifts — gifts that underscore your great concern and care for your creation. We are here in worship as gift-receivers, feeling what it is like to be so bountifully blessed. For as we discover that you would share all of the essentials of the good life, share them freely with those who desire to receive, our strivings cease, and we allow you, God, to enter our lives and to reign there joyfully. Jesus the Christ, your Son, shows us that this can indeed be so. We pray in his name. Amen.

Call to Confession
How sad that our measure of things and God's measure of things are often far apart. More tragic yet is it that we insist on our own

way — that it is right for us in our particular circumstances. So do we rationalize, and leave God out all the more; for whether we would call it such or not, we try to usurp the place of God. How vain, this exalting of self. Can we with contrite heart confess this, both to God and to one another?

Prayer of Confession
Forgive us, O God, this constant preening of self, as though our wisdom somehow surpasses yours, as though our motives and judgments are pure, more pragmatically attuned to the world in which we live than is your eternal word to us. Can we not see how far we are missing the mark? So much of what we do is predicated on greed, the desire that we get more for self though that means less for the other, though it means compromising those values we know to be God-ordained. Little wonder that the clanking of coins is an odious sound to you, O God, rather than a joyful one. Yet another sign that too often we attempt to bypass what a faith in Christ would tell us, that we might institute our own materialistic yardstick of success. Inasmuch as we can see this as folly, forgive us. This in the name of Jesus, who came as servant to truly live your way among us. Amen.

Words of Assurance
How incredible — that in spite of all of our misgivings and misdoings, God still loves us, and offers forgiveness, not partial nor qualified in any way, but complete. This must indeed come from a love that knows no limits, a desire that the final word be life, life that conquers death in all of its many forms.
What wondrous love is this — that frees us from death, that gifts us with life.

Psalter Reading (from Psalm 111)
Praise the Lord! I will give thanks to the Lord with my whole heart,
In the company of the upright, in the congregation.
Great are the works of the Lord, studied by all who delight in them.

Full of honor and majesty is his work, and his righteousness endures forever.
He has gained renown by his wonderful deeds; the Lord is gracious and merciful.
He provides food for those who revere him; he is ever mindful of his covenant.
The works of his hands are faithful and just; all his precepts are trustworthy.
They are established forever and ever, to be performed with faithfulness and uprightness.
He sent redemption to his people; he has commanded his covenant forever. Holy and awesome is his name.
The fear of the Lord is the beginning of wisdom; all who practice it have a good understanding. His praise endures forever.

Offering Sentences
God desires first that we be reconciled to our sister and brother before we lay our gift at the altar. Why? Because for gifts to be acceptable to God, they must come from pure hearts and be given with pure motives. Let us ensure that our giving measures up to this godly standard. And then let us give with joy and thanksgiving.

Prayer of Dedication
May our gifts, O God, not make an unseemly noise on the temple floor, but rather create sounds that are the sounds of caring, compassion, and concern for those in need. Let your love, Lord Jesus, direct both our giving and our living — that reconciling, healing, peacemaking, and community building be the blessed result of their use, this that your rule be known on earth as it is in heaven. Amen.

Benediction
"What does it profit you, if you gain the whole world yet lose your own soul?" A powerful lesson for this life's journey: Invest in that which in truth means life; rid yourself of those things which lead only to death. Then, in all joy and freedom LIVE!

Glory

2 Corinthians 4:3-6
Mark 8:27-33; 9:2-9

Call to Worship
God appears upon the mountain:
And commandments are given — that we might know God and know our place in community.
A sermon is given on the mount:
And beatitudes are bestowed — that we might know the love that makes us children of God.
Jesus appears transfigured on the mount:
And his person is confirmed — as Son of God and Savior.
We come to the mountain today, the mount of our worship:
And would here be affirmed in our mission and strengthened for the journey.

Invocation
God, who can behold your face, the wonder and the power which define your glory? Your presence indeed inspires a reverence that directs us to the holy. This, rather than turn us *from* everyday experiences of life, would turn us in greater comprehension *toward* them — with resources to pursue faithfully our mission as bearers of good news, as those who live with a holy zeal. So enlivened and directed by your Spirit, we pray that this hour be wisely and joyfully used as a time of praise, a time of learning, and a time of commitment anew to our calling, that of ambassador of the risen Christ. This we pray, as in awe we bow before your love, in the holiness of this moment and place, inspired by the glory of God with us. Amen.

Call to Confession
How aware of the holy are we really? Do we truly sense the glory of God to be present in all of the daily circumstances of life? And how does that affect our living? Is it an excuse for withdrawing to the mountaintop, or does it lead to an empowering for service in

the valley? Let us consider these important questions, and our answers to them, during a time of personal and corporate confession.

Prayer of Confession

Life, as we know, O God, can easily become routine, without either a sense of urgency or of joy. One week slips into another; one month goes, and the next appears without much fanfare. Life, however, if viewed as holy, can never be that way. The excitement, the glory of your presence, ever awakens those who seek new possibilities, new affirmations of faith and service. Help *us* to see; help *us* to participate in the wonder of your power here with us, available to each of us. So will every aspect of our life be given purpose and direction. We'll indeed treasure those moments when we behold your glory, but we'll equally value every moment of service that these times of inspiration and empowering make possible. Grant that we achieve this healthy rhythm to our living. It shall be so, even as we rely on your grace, your leading, O God, thankful that you are always here taking the initiative. Amen — and amen!

Words of Assurance

God is never far from us. Whether we be startled into a recognition of the holy or quietly nurtured in faith, the realization comes that God has always been there, ready to empower us with resources of grace, discernment, and spirit. As we are awakened to our need, so can we reach out and receive those very things needed for life in all its fullness, these made available as gifts of God.
Glory to God in the highest! God gifts us with life that is whole, complete in every way, eternal in God's holy presence.

Psalter Reading (from Psalm 63)

O God, you are my God, I seek you, my soul thirsts for you; my flesh faints for you, as in a dry and weary land where there is no water.
So I have looked upon you in the sanctuary, beholding your power and glory.

Because your steadfast love is better than life, my lips will praise you.
So I will bless you as long as I live; I will lift up my hands and call on your name.
My soul is satisfied as with a rich feast, and my mouth praises you with joyful lips;
For you have been my help, and in the shadow of your wings I sing for joy.

Offering Sentences

It is in the valley that we are called to serve. The fruits of our labor are an important component in this service of God and neighbor. Though God can multiply by holy love and divine power any and all of our gifts, our giving forms the base, the foundation, of what gets done for God in this place. Thus let ours be a cheerful and large-hearted giving of self — for indeed, it does make a difference.

Prayer of Dedication

You value every gift, O God, as an important contribution to your kingdom's coming on earth. For each carries with it the possibility, when combined with your love, of unlocking the heart of another, mending brokenness, providing hope and courage. Such good can come from even the smallest packages of faithfulness, if what is offered is offered freely, in your spirit, and with your will in mind. May all of our gifts be offered in this manner, this day and every day. In Jesus' name. Amen.

Benediction

Go forth from here to make known Jesus the Christ in all of his awesomeness and glory, this through a life of faithful and humble service in his name — a formidable challenge, yet truly a holy calling. With enthusiasm, great zeal, and joy be about this, your life's work. Amen.

God's Family

Ephesians 3:14-19
John 17:6-19

Call to Worship
In worship this morning we are homing.
We home in the eternal, in the family of God.
Home is where we are accepted, where we are called by name.
So do we feel that acceptance here; so does God know us by name.
Our worship in truth would make us one with God.
We come together to create this one family, a family rooted and grounded in love.

Invocation
We need to belong to a family, O God. Thus how wonderful it is to discover that we belong to yours! We need the support of someone who cares, who would help us relate to others, relate in ways that bind in harmony and build the body. Here, too, to precisely this end, you offer us your love — and would incorporate us into the body of Christ. It is within the body of Christ that we find that surrounding which prompts us to grow in spirit and in our understanding of life's true purpose. It is within the setting of Christ-inspired family that we are led to develop and to use our talents, this while shaping a community in which all are valued and peace is proclaimed. All of this, O God, you make possible, and we rejoice in it. Amen.

Call to Confession
There are, however, so many broken families around us. Ours, at times, becomes a casualty too. This occurs whenever we put self ahead of God's concern for all. We think we know better, and so we attempt to force our will upon another. Thus is the will of God denied; thus are people driven apart; thus are we separated and estranged one from the other and from God. Are we willing to

acknowledge this as a grievous and debilitating evil, and so seek God's mercy and forgiveness? Let us pray.

Prayer of Confession
We confess, O God, that we so often fail to keep Christ as center. We compromise; we water down Christ's command to show the same love to family as the holy Christ shows to us. We become more and more concerned with the well-being of self than we do with the sacrificing of self for the health of family and community. Our interests are short-sighted, and dwell more on immediate gain than on the long term building of that body which can faithfully represent Christ in the world. Restore us, O God; restore us to our true calling — that of believer in Christ, member of his family, bearer of good news to all we meet. A contrite heart, O God, you do not despise. As we surrender, so will you forgive and will guide us to depend on you more fully. Thank you, God, for your mercy; lead us forward. Amen.

Words of Assurance
In Christ all things hold together. So it is, that that which is broken is made whole again, this by a love that will not let us go. So does the Christ of God claim us yet as family, as those close to the heart of God. Thus welcome into your life that which Christ freely and gladly offers to you and to me — that in him we all might be one. **Praise be to God for granting us Christ and his healing love.**

Psalter Reading (from Psalm 107)
O give thanks to the Lord, for he is good; for his steadfast love endures forever.
He turns rivers into a desert, springs of water into thirsty ground, because of the wickedness of its inhabitants.
He turns a desert into pools of water; a parched land into springs of water.
And there he lets the hungry live, and they establish a town to live in;
They sow fields and plant vineyards, and get a fruitful yield.

By his blessing they multiply greatly, and he does not let their cattle decrease.
When they are diminished and brought low through oppression, trouble, and sorrow ...
He raises up the needy out of distress, and makes their families like flocks.
The upright see it and are glad; and all wickedness stops its mouth ...
Let those who are wise give heed to these things, and consider the steadfast love of the Lord.

Offering Sentences
Let us extend the bounds of family by means of the tithes and the offerings that we bring forward today. May what we dedicate here to God cause God's love to become real to yet others, others who yearn for affection and for a caring family to which to belong.

Prayer of Dedication
May these tithes and offerings which we dedicate to your glory, to your service, O God, open avenues of opportunities for others — that the joy we know in Christ may awaken hope in others, and that the welcome we have received into God's family be a blessing that others too may come to know and cherish. May these gifts, a part of your bounty to us, so be put to good use in your name. Amen.

Benediction
Go forth from here knowing that you belong. Cherish your roots in family. Appreciate as the great gift it is your membership in the family of God. Indeed, share this joy with others!

Hospitality

Hebrews 13:1-8, 15-16
Luke 14:1, 7-14

Call to Worship
Here within the shelter of God's holy presence do we come.
God is truly strength and protection against life's harm.
Here do we celebrate God's healing grace.
Here it is that we seek well-being for body, mind, and spirit.
We rejoice that God accepts all who come.
None is turned away; all are included in God's hospitality.
Praise be to God, for God's ways are merciful.
Praise be to God, for God's love is sure.

Invocation
Gracious and eternal God, unchanging, ever true, once again with arms opened wide you receive us into your helping, healing presence. You provide for each of us much needed respite from the storms of life which rage both within and without. We are here welcomed, and then strengthened for the journey. With a warmth that reflects your love, we come to know that we belong to something far greater than self, indeed a family widespread, from all parts, that bears your name. Thus do we rejoice and make this time one of heartfelt worship. Even as you gladly, joyfully share with us in such a complete way, may we likewise open ourselves to receive the good gifts that you bestow. In your name, above all names, do we pray. Amen.

Call to Confession
Though God seeks to meet our every need, this with mercy and an abundance that is truly amazing, we so often find pride and a lack of generosity usurping these godly traits as we confront the needs of others. We seek first a place for ourselves before we in any way show concern for our neighbor. Moreover, what we share is hardly abundance; rather, it is but a shriveled part of the whole. Let us confess to the hospitable God the many ways in which we have

failed to show hospitality, asking God's forgiveness and a redirecting for our future.

Prayer of Confession

O most holy and gracious God, your message made known to us in Jesus the Christ is clear enough: we are to share ourselves with others in the same compassionate, caring way as you share yourself with us. Rather than using our energies to seek a place for self, we are to provide welcome, acceptance, and a place at the table of life to others — to *all* others that we encounter along life's way. What an assignment that is! What a challenge! Surely we cannot do it on our own. But with the love, the insight, the strength that you both promise and provide, the story can be different. Forgive us the folly of focusing on self. Widen our vision — to include all those many others around us. Moreover, grant us the wisdom to rely on the resources that you make available to us, for they will be more than enough for both self *and* neighbor. By so doing can our lives be remade — into the compassionate, caring servants you mean us to be. Let this be done, we pray, as we hold the example of Jesus ever before us. Amen.

Words of Assurance

The patience of God is indeed amazing. The compassionate nature of God is a sure sign of God's goodness — to us. A willingness to forgive, a willingness to share, the very resources of God made available to you and to me: this is the picture of God that we can hold with confidence and assurance. Moreover, it can remake our lives! Let us rejoice in the God who cares.

Thanks be to God for not only showing the way, but for providing us the resources to walk it faithfully.

Psalter Reading (from Psalm 112)

Praise the Lord! Happy are those who revere the Lord, who greatly delight in his commandments.

Their descendants will be mighty in the land; the generation of the upright will be blessed.

Wealth and riches are in their houses, and their righteousness endures forever.
They rise in the darkness as a light for the upright; they are gracious, merciful, and righteous.
It is well with those who deal generously and lend, who conduct their affairs with justice.
For the righteous will never be moved; they will be remembered forever.
They are not afraid of evil tidings; their hearts are firm, secure in the Lord.
Their hearts are steady, they will not be afraid; in the end they will look in triumph on their foes.
They have distributed freely, they have given to the poor.
Their righteousness endures forever; their horn is exalted in honor.

Offering Sentences
Giving centers not so much on the amount as on our faithfulness in sharing what we have. This is the message that Jesus sought to impart. This is the teaching that should govern our giving, for as Jesus so demonstrated, this is the way to life in all its fullness. Let us follow that way in our living and in our giving.

Prayer of Dedication
Let these gifts carry forth your work of hospitality, O God. May they likewise involve us in ministries of hospitality — offering shelter to those who need a respite from the storms of life, holding forth healing to those wounded by the inconsiderateness of others. By this means, may some of your children, O God, find peace, this through your family acting indeed as family. In the name of the Christ, the head of the family, so be it!

Benediction
Let us depart this place of worship to be about our business as Christians — that of practicing hospitality. Let us remember that in God's sight there are no throwaway persons. Thus, let us share ourselves in Christ's name with *all* those whose paths shall this week intersect with ours. For such will be our greatest joy.

Living Stones

1 Peter 2:4-6
Matthew 16:13-20

Call to Worship
Jesus has gathered us here today, like living stones, to build the church with us.
Jesus, we feel more like shifting sands than the living stones you need.
Nonetheless, Jesus has gathered us here today, like living stones, to build the church with us.
Jesus, we feel too cracked, too broken, too impure to be useful in building a holy church.
Even so, Jesus has gathered us here today, like living stones, to build the church with us.
Jesus, though we be imperfect, we are yours. Use us in ways you devise to build your church. Amen.

Invocation
God, you know well our disposition. We enjoy privilege; we don't take so readily to responsibility. We're glad when church is comfortable; we're not so sure when it comes to us as challenge. We see tasks that need to be done, and we're thankful when someone takes the initiative — thankful that the person need not be us. God, you know well our disposition. You can easily see that we have more growing to do as your children and as disciples of the Lord Jesus Christ. May that happen this hour, we pray, as we come together as family to hear your Word, that we be energized by your Spirit, and that we commit ourselves to action in your Name. Awaken us to the joy of what we are meant to be. This we ask in Jesus' name. Amen.

Call to Confession
Do we truly wish to be awakened — awakened to things spiritual, awakened to our call that we *be* the church? Words of prayer are of little avail, unless we are ready to receive the prayer's answer.

If we pray for freedom such that we can be ourselves, be the people God means us to be, then we should not shy away from the answer that God in love provides. Let those who are prepared to receive from God so join in prayer.

Prayer of Confession

Holy God, there are days, we confess, when we would just as soon not be your church. For being the church every day makes us weary. So we ease the challenge with many a compromise. You know well that we cannot be trusted to be faithful all the time. To put it bluntly, the responsibility of having the keys to your kingdom frightens us. Already we have too much bound the good and loosed the evil. O God, save us! Save us from wanting to throw off your gentle yoke. Save us from using as an excuse, "We're only human!" Save us from practicing weakness, when instead you offer an all-sufficient strength. Save us from part time endeavor, building long vacations into attempts at service in your name. Save us, O God, and build us every day into the church you call us to be. May the example and the love of Christ so mold us and keep us focused. Amen.

Words of Assurance

Hear the word of God to the prophet Isaiah: "But those who wait for the Lord shall renew their strength, they shall mount up with wings like eagles, they shall run and not be weary, they shall walk and not faint." So does God provide for those willing to receive from this abundance of goodness and mercy.

Praise be to God, who commissions us and then provides for us, who gives us a holy task and then the resources to perform it faithfully.

Psalter Reading (from Psalm 31)

In you, O Lord, I seek refuge; do not let me ever be put to shame; in your righteousness deliver me.

Incline your ear to me; rescue me speedily, be a rock of refuge to me, a strong fortress to save me.

You are indeed my rock and my fortress; for your name's sake lead me and guide me.
Into your hand I commit my spirit; you have redeemed me, O Lord, faithful God.
I trust in you, O Lord; I say, "You are my God."
My times are in your hand. Let your face shine upon your servant; save me in your steadfast love.
Love the Lord, all you his saints. The Lord preserves the faithful.
Be strong, and let your heart take courage, all you who wait for the Lord.

Offering Sentences

Jesus so taught his disciples, "From everyone who has been given much, much will be required." Indeed, we have been given much by God. We respond to this goodness, to this extravagance of God, with lives of thanksgiving, praise, and service. This includes those tithes and offerings that we now bring forward to support the ministries of Christ's church. Let us give with joy!

Prayer of Dedication

We would be faithful to the work that you, O God, would do here in our midst. Thus do we ask that you continue to challenge us — that with compassion and with hearts burning for justice we mirror Christ's teachings and example in our daily lives, both as individuals and as that body of believers which is your church. Take what we now offer, Lord, and create from it good for many — that healing might be brought to hurt, growth to spirit, and peace to our efforts to dwell in community. All that your name be glorified. Amen.

Benediction

Each of you is a chosen instrument of God. Be that living stone, that rock-solid person of faith whom God can use to win others to life and love — so making of you and of many that community which knows God-inspired reconciliation and peace. So be it! Amen and amen!

Losing Equals Living

Mark 8:31-35
Proverbs 1:20-33

Call to Worship
We come — to praise God for life.
This is God's gift that is renewed daily.
We come — to submit ourselves to a way of life.
This is a way of life taught us patiently by Jesus the Christ.
In order to appreciate it fully we must be willing to lose it.
This is strange, yet amazing and so very fulfilling.
The purpose of our worship then is to love the Giver and the gift and to learn from both.
This we will do, as we rejoice in the presence of God this day.

Invocation
O God, your math is most unusual. Losing one's life, you say, is tantamount to saving it. We can be so protective of self that we refuse to venture forth to share ourselves with others. Thus is our life thwarted — shriveled — and becomes so much less than satisfying. Allowing life to be used, however, used for holy purposes, shapes it into a thing of beauty and great value. You, gracious God, would show us how this can be done, how this is indeed your will for each of us. Open us, we pray, that we be willing to learn your new math, and then go beyond learning to apply it to our daily living. This in faithfulness to the example of our Lord Jesus Christ, in whose name we pray. Amen.

Call to Confession
Unselfish giving always leaves us with *more*. How reluctant we are, though, to abandon ourselves completely to this principle. For it seems that we are always hoarding something for self; and not only therefore is the neighbor slighted, but we fail to learn how sufficient God's love is for every need. And so do we remain stunted in our growth. Let us ask God to free us from this unproductive way of living.

Prayer of Confession

Free us, God, from being so concerned about self. Not only does this keep us from enjoying life; it keeps us from being the person you mean us to be: ones who use gladly, in service to others, those distinctive talents that you have given us. Each of us has gifts that are meant to be shared. Yet we must risk ourselves for your sake, make ourselves vulnerable, give ourselves away, if indeed is the neighbor's need to be met. Help us to see that your love, love in abundance, makes all of this possible — if we but reach out, receive, and share. Rid us of any reluctance; shake loose from us any hesitancy. For all win, as we forget self and yield to your prompting — and so allow your Holy Spirit to work in us and through us. In truth, help us to lose our life that we might find it, our hand clasped all the while tightly in that of our Savior. So do we pray in his name. Amen.

Words of Assurance

God's love, God's mercy, God's peace never fail us. They are like the fresh dew of the morning, strength for the noon day, comforting assurance as the day draws to a close. Even as we are equipped by God for ministry, the past no longer proves a burden; the future becomes alive with possibility. This is God's way with us! Let us then with grateful hearts run with vigor and perseverance the route that God has mapped for each of us and for the life of this community of God's people.
Thanks be to God for every opportunity to serve in his name.

Psalter Reading (from Psalm 116)

I love the Lord, because he has heard my voice and my supplications.
Because he inclined his ear to me, therefore I will call on him as long as I live.
The snares of death encompassed me; the pangs of Sheol laid hold on me; I suffered distress and anguish.
Then I called on the name of the Lord: "O Lord, I pray, save my life!"
Gracious is the Lord, and righteous; our God is merciful.

The Lord protects the simple; when I was brought low, he saved me.
Return, O my soul, to your rest, for the Lord has dealt bountifully with you.
For you have delivered my soul from death, my eyes from tears, my feet from stumbling.
I walk before the Lord in the land of the living.
What shall I return to the Lord for all his bounty to me?
I will lift up the cup of salvation and call on the name of the Lord.
I will pay my vows to the Lord in the presence of all his people.

Offering Sentences
Now comes the real test. Are we willing to give ourselves away — that God be glorified, that the need of neighbor be met, that we find our own lives filled as never before with abundance? It's not that difficult — unless we make it so. We are simply to begin giving, and continue giving, leaving worry, anxiety, and any lingering doubt behind — until we truly lose ourselves in the greater purpose of God's love for the whole of creation. A lifetime of giving on this earth, and never being without. Will you join other sisters and brothers of the faith in this way of serving God?

Prayer of Dedication
God, you are pleased with every offering of the heart. For it will find its way to touch another heart, and therein create healing, friendship, community, and peace. Thus may these offerings of the heart, we pray, offerings that we bring here before you for your holy purposes, touch many another heart, and so assist in the meeting of many needs, all the while sowing in abundance the very welcome seeds of peace. As what we do is interpreted by the love of Jesus the Christ, so do we have confidence that it will be so. Amen.

Benediction
Do you really believe God's math? If so, during the week ahead use every opportunity presented to you to lose your life for the sake of the gospel. For then will you truly live. Amen!

Mother/Family

John 13:31-35
1 Corinthians 13:4-8a, 13

Call to Worship
We gather as the family of God to worship.
For God has so blessed us with home and family.
It is here that we find lessons for life and the joy of living together.
It is here that words are authenticated by deeds, enabling both communion and community.
Central to the family's well-being is the love of mother and father.
Today we remember the role of mother, and in worship praise the dedication and the patience that mark a mother's devotion.

Invocation
God, full of caring, full of wisdom, you establish us in families — that love and laughter, that understanding and trust might bless the lives of all of earth's children. You would have your peace cultivated in this way among us — that in such intimacy of sharing all will know full growth of being and full breadth and depth of relationship. Of great importance is the mother's contribution to the health and harmony of family life. We praise today all mothers — their difficult role, yet the faithfulness of so many in performing it. Blessed are those mothers who lean on you, and there find both the strength and the wisdom for each day's journey. Thank you, God, for the many evidences of your guidance and mercy. So guide us now in this hour of worship. Amen.

Call to Confession
Too often families are fragmented, even Christian families. Love and laughter turn to mistrust and words spoken in anger. Peace becomes brokenness. For all of us are human, and humans are sinful. If in humbleness of spirit we are willing to confess this, then there is yet hope. For God grants forgiveness; and with forgiveness, healing; and with healing, renewal of mind and spirit, such that all things may once again be bound together in love. Let us so confess our needs.

Prayer of Confession

We would have this festival of the Christian home, O God, be truly a time of celebration. Indeed, in our homes we have known blessing upon blessing. We have known your presence there in the love and faithful dedication of parents. Moreover, we have attempted to convey that same love, that same dedication to our children. We have tried, O Lord. We have really tried! Yet we must confess those times when trying was not enough, when we needed help from another source, when however we failed to turn to you. All along we knew that you were with us and for us; still we refused to reach out to accept the hand that you extended. Let that change. Let that change now. God, you say that there is yet time — for forgiveness, for healing, for renewal, for the enriching of family. Guide us that this become the great good news that it can be — for every family. So do we pray, relying on your love and on your mercy. Amen.

Words of Assurance

Like the mother who so desperately pled with Jesus that her daughter be healed, might we too hear the words of our Savior as he replied, "Woman, how great is your faith! Go, your daughter is well!" For thus is God's healing power made available to all who in trust believe. So do all in the family benefit from God's constant care.
Praise be to God! God values each one of us and ever seeks to bind us together as family.

A Reading from Proverbs — honoring faithful homemakers (from Proverbs 31)

A capable wife, who can find? She is far more precious than jewels.
The heart of her husband trusts her, and he will have no lack of gain.
She does him good, and not harm, all the days of her life.
She seeks wool and flax, and works with willing hands.
She rises while it is still night and provides food for her household ...
She girds herself with strength, and makes her arms strong.
Her lamp does not go out at night.
She opens her hand to the poor, and reaches out her hands to the needy.

Strength and dignity are her clothing, and she laughs at the time to come.
She opens her mouth with wisdom, and the teaching of kindness is on her tongue.
She looks well to the ways of her household, and does not eat the bread of idleness.
Her children rise up and call her blessed; her husband too, and he praises her:
"Many women have done excellently, but you surpass them all."
Charm is deceitful, and beauty is vain, but a woman who fears the Lord is to be praised.

Offering Sentences

Grateful hearts are not silent hearts. They are busy proclaiming and living God's Word, that all in the family might benefit. One way to so live the Word is in the joyful sharing with others of those resources which God has placed at our disposal. For the family's health and further growth, let us share this morning in cheerfulness and gratitude, asking that God direct these gifts to those particular scenes of greatest need.

Prayer of Dedication

God, you who are the great Provider of the human family, accept these contributions that we now make to family. May they be used to strengthen the ties that bind us as one. Wherever there is need, let us in love assess that need, and then reach out in your name with the resources entrusted to us, sharing gladly and liberally with family, neighbor, and stranger. Let us begin now — for we do have much that we can give. All because of your love shown to us in Jesus Christ, he whom we affirm as Savior and head of family. Amen.

Benediction

Honor your mother, today and every day. Bless your family, by contributing to it many and varied acts of love. And praise God, who enables all, and faithfully stands by your side. So will you begin to discover what God's peace can mean to you and to the world around you. Amen!

New Year/New Beginnings

Isaiah 43:15-21
2 Corinthians 5:16-21

Call to Worship
There are times for new beginnings,
And for renewing ministries.
The old must be left behind, unworthy things cast off.
There must likewise be an openness to receive the new, the untried yet full of promise.
What will we make of the new, that the new year brings?
With great expectations, we let God mold us afresh, that we be fit instruments for new avenues of service in God's name.

Invocation
Holy God, it is here in worship that we finally take time to reflect upon the new year — to consider what it offers and what it demands. In one sense, it is no more than one month sliding over into another. Yet the very fact that we invest it with something new causes us in mind and heart to assess where we've been and where we are going. And this is good. For we can then pray, O God, that you help us get rid of any excess baggage that we've been carrying along. Purge us, we ask, of all that holds us back, that keeps us from maturing into the people of God you mean us to be. Freed of unwanted weights and with high expectations, may we then venture forth to accomplish great things in your name. Amen.

Call to Confession
One of our heaviest weights is that of apathy, that there is a sameness to each day, a droning on of life, in which there is nothing new under the sun. The potential that Christmas offered — the urgent need of the neighbor, our own need to grow in spirit — none of this has stirred us. God calls, and would have us truly make a difference, yet there is no zeal, no purpose to our busyness. Let us confess our need, and pray that God inspires us to action worthy of a follower of Jesus Christ.

Prayer of Confession
What will it take, O God, to set us on fire? We are so comfortable! Frankly, we fail to see the necessity of getting fired up, fired up about another's need, for the other is a stranger to us, and we labor hard enough to meet our own needs. Yet we know that we're not true disciples unless we do *something*. Indeed, the feeling of having failed you gnaws at us at times, that is, until with our rationalizing minds we brush such feeling aside. It is thus with some trepidation that we say: Confront us, O God, with the power of your Word. Let the searing light of your love burn deep within our heart and awaken us to our calling, that indispensable work that you would have us do lest another die. May the new year indeed bring something new into our lives — first, the surprise that we are forgiven; then, a commission that we love as we have been loved; and finally, a joy, that following you, even sacrificing for you, we shall find ourselves serving others, others that we've never known before, so creating friendship and community and peace. Such is your will for us. We pray that we burn with your love and with your zeal. Amen.

Words of Assurance
Listen to the Christ as he says, "See, I am making all things new." To those thirsty for life, life that is fulfilling and lasting, our Lord gives water as a gift from the spring of the water of life. Indeed, if anyone is in Christ, that person is a new creation. The old has passed away; everything, yes everything, has been made new. So are we fired with the glory of God and take up our work as messengers, as reconcilers, as those sent on a holy mission by the Almighty.
Thanks be to God for the gift of Christ that forgives, renews, and empowers.

Psalter Reading (from Psalm 29)
Ascribe to the Lord, O heavenly beings, ascribe to the Lord glory and strength.
Ascribe to the Lord the glory of his name; worship the Lord in holy splendor.
The voice of the Lord is over the waters; the God of glory thunders, the Lord, over mighty waters.

The voice of the Lord is powerful; the voice of the Lord is full of majesty.
The voice of the Lord flashes forth flames of fire.
The voice of the Lord shakes the wilderness; the Lord shakes the wilderness of Kadesh.
The voice of the Lord causes the oaks to whirl, and strips the forest bare;
And in his temple all say, "Glory!"
May the Lord give strength to his people!
May the Lord bless his people with peace!

Offering Sentences
The magi pondered carefully what gifts might be appropriate for the child of God they sought to visit. And what they chose was indeed fitting — for the occasion and for their worship. What gifts have you chosen today — to reflect your devotion, your commitment to Christ and his way? Consider with care how you will serve, for this will have great influence not only on your life but on the lives of others around you. Come, let us worship the Lord with our offerings, the first fruits of our Christmas joy.

Prayer of Dedication
What wondrous love is this — so wondrous that we too are allowed to share it wherever we go. Even as these gifts represent devotion kindled anew, so may our walk through the new year challenge us with many an opportunity for service and call forth from us the best that we are, this, that the whole of the world around us be built up in love. So can it be, with Christ among us and in us. In his name, we ask this. Amen.

Benediction
Know that God has invested glory in this new year that we've entered, not in some general sense, but in a very specific way for you and for me. Moreover, Jesus is present to fan it to flame. Why would we settle for less? Let us thank God for such high expectations and for the Christ who stands by our side to bring what we think impossible to pass. So let the new year — and our service in it — begin! Amen and amen!

Open Hands

Luke 7:36—8:3

Call to Worship
An open hand, bestowing the bounty of creation.
So do we know you as Creator, O God.
Open hands, nailed to the cross in love.
So do we know you as Savior, O God.
An open hand, extended to us in friendship.
So do we know you as Holy Spirit, O God.
We too would worship you with open hands.
Holding nothing as our own, but offering all to you.

Invocation
You teach us, as the God who gives and gives again, that the way truly to hold onto life is — with open hands. Too often we try to hang on with fists clenched, reluctant to turn loose for fear of losing, losing that for which we have labored so diligently and so long. So do we clutch, clasp, and grasp, all the while turning inward, causing life to shrink rather than expand. You proclaim that life, O God, has quite a different meaning, that it finds its purpose and is fulfilled only as we turn loose and give ourselves away. Let that be our focus this hour, we pray, and in our worship of you discover life in all of its splendor and glory. In the name of Christ, who with open hands offered himself that we might live. Amen.

Call to Confession
All of us have our particular and peculiar ways of hanging on. We have heard God's call to turn loose, yet can find neither the desire nor the strength to comply fully. Can't we see that we are much the poorer because of this failure to grow in spirit? Let us ask God to open eyes, mind, heart, and finally our hands — that we learn how much better life can be as we let go and let God.

Prayer of Confession

Gracious God, help us to shake ourselves free — that we cling not to self but rather trust in you. We are so prone to define what is "mine" that we allow little room for neighbor, for family, or even for you, O God. Self and things for self become all consuming. So do we insulate and isolate ourselves from others — and from life. No wonder that "life," as we view it within our own narrow dimensions, becomes less than fulfilling, indeed often drives us to disappointment and despair. God, forgive us this smallness, this provincialism, this selfishness. Though you have lo these many centuries proclaimed the true meaning of life — hands open, bestowing, sacrificing, loosing all for us — may we at last awaken to the fact that you mean for us to follow the same pattern too, that we enjoy fullness of life in a total sharing of life. With your love prompting us, Lord it can be so. May it be so *today*. Amen.

Words of Assurance

God not only gives us a pattern for living, but also resources and encouragement which enable us faithfully to make the pattern our own. Thus, we can know life in all its fullness. All is a gift of God's love, a love that in costly fashion is revealed to us in the life, death, and resurrection of Jesus Christ. Though impossible for us to achieve by the strength of our own labors, this great gift is nonetheless bestowed upon all who would receive it, this because of God's concern and care for each one of us, Christ's open hands that even now embrace us and bring us peace.
Thanks be to God for a gift beyond measure, one that means life for us all.

Psalter Reading (from Psalm 32)

Happy are those whose transgression is forgiven, whose sin is covered.
Happy are those to whom the Lord imputes no iniquity, and in whose spirit there is no deceit.
While I kept silence, my body wasted away through my groaning all day long.
For day and night your hand was heavy upon me; my strength was dried up as by the heat of summer.

Then I acknowledged my sin to you and I did not hide my iniquity.
I said, "I will confess my transgressions to the Lord," and you forgave the guilt of my sin.
Therefore let all who are faithful offer prayer to you; at a time of distress, the rush of mighty waters shall not reach them.
You are a hiding place for me; you preserve me from trouble; you surround me with glad cries of deliverance.
Be glad in the Lord and rejoice, O righteous.
And shout for joy, all you upright of heart.

Offering Sentences

A definite way to determine whether the hand is clenched or open is to observe your response at this point in our worship each Sunday, as gifts are presented to sustain God's work on this earth. Have we indeed been freed enough by God's grace to give freely? God's grace certainly is sufficient. But have we received it without condition into our living? We answer, as in an act of worship we bring and consecrate tithes and offerings.

Prayer of Dedication

Help us more and more, O God, to know the joy of giving, the assurance that we are here building up lives, fitting them for service in your name. Hope here takes precedence over despair. Sharing is shown to be more satisfying than selfishness. Hurt is healed. Aimlessness becomes life lived with purpose and zeal. All because we are learning, God, to let your love be administered by open hands, hands that truly help rather than hinder. We do this, with Christ as our guide. Amen.

Benediction

Pay attention to your hands during the days of this new week. How often are they fists clenched tightly, reluctant to turn loose of that which could mean life for another? How often are they open — to receive another into God's care, an action that will bless you both? Make your assessment; and whatever it be, ask God to guide you to yet further growth. For God is good; God's love is ever present and full. Amen!

Palm Sunday

John 12:12-19

Call to Worship
We welcome Jesus to Jerusalem — and into our sanctuary.
Yes, let us give the Savior a festive welcome!
Not only do we welcome him into our place of worship; we welcome him into our hearts.
May our worship so reflect such a devotion and loyalty.
For we enter a Holy Week, with much of significance to our faith still to come.
May we chart a path through the week that will indeed cause our faith to grow.
There is, we find, both good news and sad news to proclaim.
By God's grace, the good news shall prevail, and we shall be proclaimers of it.

Invocation
This is a bittersweet Sunday for us, O God. We are eager to join in the celebration, for in truth there is good news in the Messiah's coming. Yet we know from past history how quickly hosannas can turn into hostile shouts of angry, confused people. We will go that route again this week. Guide us, we pray, in our times of worship and in our daily walk that we emerge from the journey a stronger people, our faith energized and deepened, our actions more fully attuned to your holy will. May our worship now so inspire us to begin this special time in the presence of our Savior. It is in his name that we pray. Amen.

Call to Confession
This is a week when we try desperately to shift the blame. For surely we want to have no part in the killing of the Son of God. We remember, however, the words of the early Christian John: "If we say that we have no sin, we deceive ourselves, and the truth is not in us." Also we remember that not only Judas but all the rest of the twelve responded, "Is it I, Lord?" when Jesus declared that one of

them would betray him. Thus, let each of us come before God and confess our sins, those ways in which we too deny God's Son and so contribute to his crucifixion. For only by so doing can we know forgiveness, hope, and the newness of resurrection.

Prayer of Confession
Ours, O God, is not an open hostility toward Jesus. Rather, it is a lack of fervor, a desire *not* to be involved, an apathy on our part. Even as we would not be part of the Good Friday mob, so do we prefer not to be seen as part of the crowd that accompanied Jesus in Palm Sunday celebration. Indeed, when has our worship of late been true celebration? When of late have we shown ourselves willing to follow one who so radically shares love, imparts justice, and preaches peace? By our lukewarmness have we contributed to the nailing of Jesus to the cross. As was spoken long ago, "Would that you were either hot or cold!" But instead, we have been tepid. Forgive us, O God, you who are so gracious and so patient. Call us this Holy Week to a true appreciation of your Son's sacrifice and what it means for each of us. Prepare us for Easter in its full glory, the transforming power that it can introduce into our living. This we ask in the courageous and saving name of Jesus, who gave all for our well-being. Amen.

Words of Assurance
Hear those most familiar words of scripture; hear them and take them to heart: "God so loved the world that he gave his only begotten Son, that whosoever believes in him should not perish but have everlasting life." Indeed, eternal life is God's gift through Christ to each of us. Will we with grateful hearts and willing spirits receive the gift?
Yes, we do receive it, ever praise God for it, and so seek to imitate by word and deed Christ's life of loving and faithful service.

Psalter Reading (from Psalm 118)
Let Israel say, "His steadfast love endures forever."
Open to me the gates of righteousness, that I may enter through them and give thanks to the Lord.

This is the gate of the Lord; the righteous shall enter through it.
I thank you that you have answered me and have become my salvation.
The stone that the builders rejected has become the chief cornerstone.
This is the Lord's doing; it is marvelous in our eyes.
This is the day that the Lord has made; let us rejoice and be glad in it.
Save us, we beseech you, O Lord! O Lord, we beseech you, give us success!
Blessed is the one who comes in the name of the Lord. We bless you from the house of the Lord.
The Lord is God, and he has given us light. Bind the festal procession with branches, up to the horns of the altar.
You are my God, and I will give thanks to you; you are my God, I will extol you.
O give thanks to the Lord, for he is good, for his steadfast love endures forever.

Offering Sentences

The supreme gift is that of life itself. Would that we at this time be ready to offer our lives, that others might live. For by offering our lives, we do not lose them; rather, we find them. God would not only match our gift, but in every way exceed it, that our lives truly be lives of abundance. Let us gladly share these riches — that all have enough, and that all come to know the goodness of our Lord.

Prayer of Dedication

Enable these gifts, O God, to do the work of the cross: healing, reconciling, affirming, and sending forth in mission. You value each gift and giver — and we in turn know the joy of helping others in ways crucial to their well-being. Even as the cross gave way to an empty tomb, so may acts of redemption among us cause new beginnings. Use each gift, O loving God, to the max, just as you used your Son's life to the max. And may the results be just as glorious! In your holy name do we ask it. Amen.

Benediction

The journey has begun. Where will it take you this week? Hopefully, to a Table spread for all humankind, to a Hill with a wretched yet saving cross, and to the Dawn of a new day, one where life truly sparkles and shall go on and on forever and ever. Such is the way of God. Let us follow it. Amen!

Peace

John 14:23-29
2 Corinthians 4:13-18

Call to Worship
God offers us peace as a gift.
It is not for us to make; rather, it is for us to receive.
With peace comes purpose, a calling to life and to love.
We find this purpose in Christ, flowing from the peace he bestows.
Thus is community built, with each member a valued part of the whole.
So would we find community here, among this group of God's people.
Praise be to God; we all belong.
Gifting us with peace, God makes us complete in every way.

Invocation
O God, wise and caring, you remove all fear from our living. Confident about our future, complete in our knowledge of the way, daily immersed in such communion as can come only from a deep sense of belonging — all of these blessings are real because you have so gifted us with peace. Truly it is a gift that the world cannot give; yet out of the abundance of your love all things become possible, and with them this greatest gift of all. As we worship today, help us, O God, to value all the more the gift by learning afresh how it can radically change our lives for the good. Help us to know that you are there for us at all times. We are never alone. There is nothing to fear! Praise to you, O God, for the gift of peace. Amen.

Call to Confession
Challenges come, confronting us and our faith. Yet rather than allow the peace of God to flood our thoughts and actions, rather than trust God to supply all of that needed to take us safely through and cause us to grow, we instead rely on our meager resources;

and when these prove insufficient, we fear, we despair, we consider ourselves abandoned and alone. God, even so, stands by our side with the gift of peace in hand. It is ours, says God, if with humble and repentant spirit we would but receive it. Let us with right heart and mind and action do just that.

Prayer of Confession

All striving on our part to preserve self leads, O God, to but further fear, further feelings of incompleteness, further sense of isolation. We try so hard to make peace — for our inner selves, and for our outer selves in community. Why do we not recognize that you are present, offering us as gift the very thing we yearn for? Is it that we fail to take it because we fear there may be strings attached? Or, is it a matter of our own troublesome will still getting in the way? Forgive us all of these impediments that we place in the way of life. Assist us, we pray, that we might remove them and know in full measure your peace — the gift it is and the blessings that it brings — this, that our lives might be whole, as you mean them to be. We do ask this in the name of Christ Jesus, he who came to present us the gift and to show us the way. Amen.

Words of Assurance

Hear the words of Jesus: "I came that they may have life, and have it abundantly." Such is the will of God for us. Such is the power of holy love. God, in offering peace, includes with it forgiveness. So are we assured that we belong to the family of God, every last one of us who desires to be.
Let us receive with thanksgiving this wondrous blessing of our God.

Psalter Reading (from Psalm 85)

Show us your steadfast love, O Lord, and grant us your salvation.
Let me hear what God the Lord will speak,
For he will speak peace to his people, to his faithful, to those who turn to him in their hearts.
Surely his salvation is at hand for those who revere him, that his glory may dwell in our land.

Steadfast love and faithfulness will meet; righteousness and peace will kiss each other.
Faithfulness will spring up from the ground, and righteousness will look down from the sky.
The Lord will give what is good, and our land will yield its increase.
Righteousness will go before him, and will make a path for his steps.

Offering Sentences
If a person knows the peace of belonging, then sharing is easy. All those around are part of one grand family, and the well-being of the whole family becomes paramount. All are needed; all find their special place of service. Each person's contribution is valued. Treasuring this fact that we belong, let us with joyful spirit bring forth and dedicate offerings — that this part of God's family be sustained and upbuilt in love.

Prayer of Dedication
All things have their proper place in your tapestry of life, O God. Thus is there a wholeness, a completeness, a peacefulness to your work among us. May what we now bring before you as our gifts of love be so directed by your Spirit that they take their rightful place in that piece of the tapestry which is ours to compose and color and complete. This, for the fulfillment of your joyous and redeeming work on this earth. In Jesus' name and with his example ever before us. Amen.

Benediction
Indeed, may God's peace like a river water our parched souls and uphold us each day, that whatever the circumstances may be, we shall know that it is well with our souls. Thus is fear banished and the peace of God's love revealed in all its fullness. Amen!

Power

John 6:56-69
Ephesians 6:10-17

Call to Worship
God of power and might,
God of love and mercy,
Your power challenges and changes;
Your power guides and fulfills.
God's power equates with justice and mercy.
So is God worthy of honor and praise.
Let our worship express this.
Let our lives mirror the same.

Invocation
God, your Spirit of power leads to life. In the struggle between forces of good and evil, light and darkness, it is your power that introduces justice and mercy. It is your power that perseveres until life in every way is the victor over death. Central to your exercise of power, healing and reconciliation serve to build a way of living together that can truly lead to peace, a peace that endures. So do we come to honor in worship your way of acting in our midst, your use of power, and to pattern our lives in such a manner as to represent you faithfully in all of our relationships of both this day and tomorrow. This we pray in the name of Jesus, who indeed makes it possible. Amen.

Call to Confession
Selfish misuse of power plagues all aspects of life around us. Family, community, our own well-being are all threatened; and we can easily shift the blame to another. We, however, must bear our share of responsibility. Let us, therefore, carefully examine our relationships, in what and in whom we place our trust, and so determine how power is used and shared. Let us confess wherein we have misused and have sought to manipulate relationships — that we ready heart and mind to be guided in God's ways of power and peace.

Prayer of Confession
Too often, Lord, we stand firm in our own misguided perception of power. Rather than submit to your use of power, which aims always to upbuild in love, we pursue our own selfish interest, gaining whatever allies we can along the way. What emerges is not closely-knit community where the well-being of all is paramount, but rather individuals in isolation easily swayed by swift and tortuous currents of personal glory, greed, and gain. Forgive us these selfish outbursts, O God, this use of power for self alone rather than for all. Instill within us a new spirit, one willing to bow to your will and way. Educate us and convert us to that way, for we ask it in the name of him who is the Way, the Truth, and the Life, one of great power, yet one who ever uses power wisely and compassionately. It is in his name, the name of Jesus the Christ, that we pray. Amen.

Words of Assurance
May we too with Peter respond to Jesus: "Lord, to whom can we go? You have the words of eternal life. We have come to believe and know that you are the Holy One of God." Indeed, it is Christ who opens us to life and grants us his power, his kind of power, his understanding of power, to live life to the fullest.
To Jesus we render our thanks; to Jesus we commit our living.

Psalter Reading (from Psalm 86)
Incline your ear, O Lord, and answer me, for I am poor and needy.
Preserve my life, for I am devoted to you; save your servant who trusts in you.
Gladden the soul of your servant, for to you, O Lord, I lift up my soul.
For you, O Lord, are good and forgiving, abounding in steadfast love to all who call on you.
There is none like you among the gods, O Lord, nor are there any works like yours.
For you are great and do wondrous things; you alone are good.
Teach me your way, O Lord, that I may walk in your truth; give me an undivided heart to revere your name.

I give thanks to you, O Lord, my God, with my whole heart, and I will glorify your name forever.

Offering Sentence
Our offering to God is best demonstrated in how we care for one another. The community that shows forth justice and compassion for all of its members has truly offered to God that gift most pleasing to the Almighty. Let us work toward that end by means of the gifts that we bring forth at this time.

Prayer of Dedication
God, use these gifts, we pray, to make known your power, a power that heals and unites, a power that builds up in love and sustains in peace, a power that perseveres until all are included, a power that endures through time even unto eternity. May not only these offerings but every talent be dedicated to this use of power. So do we find our example in Christ. We pray, looking to him. Amen.

Benediction
Put on the whole armor of God — that you may remain faithful in your service to God. Go in peace, for the God of peace will sustain you and will bring your good work to fruition — that your life be joy beyond measure. All of this is within God's power to will and to accomplish. Praise, honor, and glory be to God — that his Word indeed accomplishes that which it is sent forth into the world to do.

Pruning

John 15:1-8
1 John 4:16b-21

Call to Worship
We come to worship Jesus the Christ.
He is the vine from whom we draw our sustenance.
Being the branches, we are dependent upon him in every way.
Thus are we fed and are able to bear fruit.
This is the plan of the vinegrower, who has planted the vine for a purpose.
The vinegrower is God, the one who provides, the one who also judges.
Our worship confirms God's plan for our lives.
Our worship indeed confirms how we are to live: as ones who abide in Christ.

Invocation
Rather than *cut off*, we are thankful, O God, that we are *attached to*. You include us — as part of your nurturing of creation. You feed us each day that we might in turn produce good fruit and so be able to feed others. Our only real sustenance is from you. Our health is totally dependent upon our willingness to attach ourselves completely to that life support which is Word and Spirit. May our worship today instill within us that desire. May what we do here cause good fruit to be formed. This in Christ's name and by the power of his holy love. Amen.

Call to Confession
We know that vines need pruning to produce well. That which is nonproductive must be removed in order that new, hearty growth can occur. So it is with our lives. *We* need pruning — to rid ourselves of that which is ineffectual and empty of value, that our lives might be useful and of worth to God and our neighbor. Are we ready to ask God to prune us? For the moment we may indeed feel some pain, but then exhilaration and joy. Will you join me?

Prayer of Confession
God, you know better than we what needs lopping off. We submit ourselves to whatever vine surgery you may find it necessary to perform. For we realize that all is done with the greatest of care — that we be shaped into able, life-giving purveyors of your Word and Spirit. So instill within us, we ask, renewed fervor and zeal, that we produce fruit worthy of the good news we are to represent. For thus will our focus be lifted beyond self to that which we may share with family, friend, and stranger. And so will we be doing our part in the uniting of all of creation within your single purpose of love and peace. Prune us, shape us, direct us, use us — that we truly abide in you, and by our faithful response serve you in helpful ways. This in the name of Christ. Amen.

Words of Assurance
God's love is always at work for our well-being. Whether it be pruning, or causing us to bud and blossom, or nurturing us that fruit be formed in abundance, all is evidence of God's gracious care — available to each of us, without exception. Let us with gratefulness of heart accept all that God has in store for us.
Thanks be to God — for so patiently molding us, that we be faithful and productive children of the Most High.

Psalter Reading (from Psalm 22)
From you comes my praise in the great congregation; my vows I will pay before those who revere him.
The poor shall eat and be satisfied; those who seek him shall praise the Lord. May your hearts live forever!
All the ends of the earth shall remember and turn to the Lord; and all the families of the nations shall worship before him.
For dominion belongs to the Lord, and he rules over the nations.
To him, indeed, shall all who sleep in the earth bow down;
Before him shall bow all who go down to the dust, and I shall live for him.
Posterity will serve him; future generations will be told about the Lord,

And proclaim his deliverance to a people as yet unborn, saying that he has done it.

Offering Sentences

What better means of giving evidence of good fruit than by the tithes and offerings we now bring forward for God's work in this place. Let this be done as a joyful expression of who we are as God's people and of what we propose to do *in his name* with our lives. May much good fruit by this means be shared — that hopes be raised and unity be our witness to all around.

Prayer of Dedication

Each gift of love here offered is, O God, a sign of your presence in this place. May our continuing commitment here be translated into a faithful witness of words and a host of caring deeds. Let much good fruit be the mark of this congregation. It will be so, even as we depend upon you each day in all of our doing. Amen.

Benediction

Remember always that Christ is the vine. We have the good fortune of being the branches, that is, if we abide *in him*, if we purposely cast our lot with him for the whole of life. We have *all* to gain — or *all* to lose. Which will it be, dear friend? My advice to you, my prayer for you: Choose Christ, and so find yourself in a position truly to live.

Responsibility

James 1:23-25
Luke 10:25-37

Call to Worship
God as Creator provides order and abundance.
So are we called to be responsible stewards of God's creation.
God as Redeemer provides forgiveness and newness of life.
So are we called to give thanks to God and to broadcast the good news.
God as Sustainer provides wisdom, courage, and strength.
So are we called to serve others diligently and with compassion.
Let us then worship God as Creator, Redeemer, and Sustainer.
So may our faith reflect good stewardship, an exuberant witness, and humble service.

Invocation
Ever present and active God, you likewise urge us to be doers of the Word and not hearers only. You yourself were not content until the Word became flesh and dwelt among us, full of grace and truth. Jesus, your Son, through actions and service and sacrifice thereby created those very conditions wherein we might be at peace with you and with those around us. You would thus not only save us, but enable us to be responsible children of the Most High, doers of your Word. Help us so to view life as a means of growing, through a giving of self and through active participation in the well-being of community. May your presence in our worship this day guide us further as Word in truth becomes deed. Amen.

Call to Confession
Words in our culture are cheap. Actions — faithful and responsible actions — are more costly. Many times we opt for the words and shirk the actions. The result is predictable: brokenness, lack of trust, loss of hope. And through it all, do we even sense that *we* are the culprits? Let us recognize our complicity, our duplicity, and our need for renewal of spirit and a pledging afresh of commitment.

Prayer of Confession

How many times, O God, have we known the right and responsible thing to do, yet have allowed the occasion to pass without the response that was sorely needed? We excuse ourselves by saying that it is too risky to get "involved." Our neighbor thus lacks what we with our God-given talents could have provided. We nod assent to great words of faith, but then beg off when we are asked to apply those words to a lifestyle that is Christ-like. We come to ask forgiveness, yet asking forgiveness, we realize, is but the first step. It alone is too little. We need both forgiveness *and* a zeal to pursue in deed what we are meant to be. Merciful God, meet with your grace, we pray, both of these needs. Awaken us to opportunities for service that are ever around us, and hold us accountable as children of the Way, the Truth, and the Life. So would we follow Jesus. It is in his strength, the strength of his love at work, that we pray. Amen.

Words of Assurance

"Once you were no people, but now you are God's people. Once you had not received mercy, but now you have received mercy — this that you may proclaim the mighty acts of him who called you out of darkness into his marvelous light." And more than proclaim, we are to live this same word into deed in our daily living.
Thanks be to God for this challenge, for this further call to service.

Psalter Reading (from Psalm 19)

The law of the Lord is perfect, reviving the soul;
The decrees of the Lord are sure, making wise the simple;
The precepts of the Lord are right, rejoicing the heart;
The commandment of the Lord is clear, enlightening the eyes;
The fear of the Lord is pure, enduring forever;
The ordinances of the Lord are true and righteous altogether.
More to be desired are they than gold, even much fine gold:
Sweeter also than honey, and drippings of the honeycomb.
Moreover by them is your servant warned;
In keeping them there is great reward.

Let the words of my mouth
And the meditation of my heart
Be acceptable to you, O Lord,
My rock and my redeemer.

Offering Sentences
Every Sunday we are presented at this point in our worship with an opportunity to serve — to be a doer of the Word. Our tithes and offerings bring the love of Christ and renewed hope not only to those within the congregation, but to people in need within our community and to folk the world over, this in very concrete and practical ways. How much is enough? Let your heart, your talents, and your commitment to Christ provide the answer.

Prayer of Dedication
As we return this part of your creation to you, O God, we look to your wisdom, your compassion, your righteousness for guidance in its use — this that good news become real in the lives of others, moreover, that understanding, community, and peace emerge in places where heretofore discord, selfishness, and indifference have ruled in the hearts and lives of people. O Christ, let your love break forth wherever humble service is rendered in your name. Amen.

Benediction
Yes, we are responsible — responsible to God, responsible for the children of God around us. Let us then not hesitate, but be doers of the Word of God, accepting gladly the call to be servant, faithful in every way to our neighbor, as we ever expand the definition of neighbor to include all of humanity, indeed all of creation. Amen!

The Risen Christ

John 21:1-19

Call to Worship
God is never far from any of us.
Indeed, God is very present, at all times and in all places.
It is an affirming, guiding presence, enabling and supportive.
Thus we should call upon God and welcome God into our lives.
Let us seek that presence this hour, and see how the risen Christ would appear to us.
Let us be prepared for him to enter our lives, and bless us with his kind of power.

Invocation
God of mercy, God of grace, ever living, ever near, you come to us rather than wait for us to come to you. You are available — and have resources to meet our every need. It is for us to recognize this, and then to welcome you for who you are, as one who bestows life and love. May our worship this hour lead to this sort of recognition and welcome, a true celebration of people with their God. Enliven our spirits with your Holy Spirit, that we become bearers of good news, that of resurrection, new beginnings, faithful testimony to your work among us. So be it. Amen.

Call to Confession
Even though God stands before us, even though God is here in our midst, we find it difficult to recognize this God. God's Holy Spirit, God's divine power, would assist us that we meet in positive fashion each challenge of this life, yet we fail to take into our lives gifts of God so freely and liberally offered. We limp along, when in truth we could be growing — in faith, in word, and in deed. Let us ask God in prayer that our eyes be opened, that we see and savor the good that God has for each of us.

Prayer of Confession

Just as the disciples saw a figure on the shore that they could not at first recognize, we too sense that a power is present here, one that would help us rather than oppose us, yet we hesitate to call it by name. So do we miss the best that you, God, would offer us. We daily struggle with our problems, when in truth help stands right by our side. When will we wise up, open our eyes, and see? Christ, you never force yourself upon us, yet you have for us the very nourishment that we need for body, spirit, and soul. May we, like Peter, on recognizing you be so overcome by joy that we immediately approach you and pledge to you our love and our loyalty, never again to leave you in this life or in the next. So awaken us today, we pray, that our future be powerfully and inexorably changed — for the good. This we ask in the name of the Risen One, our Advocate and Friend. Amen.

Words of Assurance

The risen Christ motions to us to come, to enjoy his presence, and to be nourished by the life-giving food that he offers. It is indeed freely given, yet it calls for a faithful response. It is there in abundance, yet we are called to share it with all, all who hunger and like ourselves need to be spiritually renewed. Let us not hold back; Christ means to share with you and with me, until we all be filled. **With joy we recognize the Christ and all that he offers. Thanks be to God for such a gracious and filling gift.**

Psalter Reading (from Psalm 30)

I will extol you, O Lord, for you have drawn me up, and did not let my foes rejoice over me.
O Lord my God, I cried to you for help, and you have healed me.
O Lord, you brought up my soul from Sheol.
You restored me to life from among those gone down to the Pit.
Sing praises to the Lord, O you his faithful ones, and give thanks to his holy name.
For his anger is but for a moment; his favor is for a lifetime.

Weeping may linger for the night, but joy comes in the morning.
You have turned my mourning into dancing; you have taken off my sackcloth and clothed me with joy.
This that my soul may praise you and not be silent.
O Lord my God, I will give thanks to you forever.

Offering Sentences
With Christ, a little turns into much. With Christ, there is no hesitancy about offering to another in love. Christ says to each, "Follow me." So, let us follow his example in our giving and in our service, and we will be amazed at how our little can grow — and grow — and become much. Let us present to God our tithes and our offerings on this day of resurrection.

Prayer of Dedication
For every gift dedicated in love there is a purpose. God, we ask you to show us the purposes for these gifts, those useful ways in which they may be employed to accomplish your will in places near and far. We bow to your wisdom and guidance, O God. May we be perceptive enough to interpret it aright and faithful enough to act upon it. In Jesus' name. Amen.

Benediction
The risen Christ stands beckoning. To each of us he offers those same words as he spoke to Simon Peter: "Follow me." Let us too reply, "Lord, you know that I love you." And then let us authenticate our words with our deeds and follow faithfully. Amen!

Sabbath

Isaiah 58:9b-14
Luke 13:10-17

Call to Worship
Indeed, this is a day of rest and gladness.
This is God's Sabbath, created for our reflection and renewal.
Let us then not profane it, but keep it holy.
We do this as we honor God and commit ourselves to the well-being of God's creation.
Each of us individually needs a personal rejuvenation of spirit.
Together we seek a strengthening of community, a community that continues to build itself in love.
So do we come as one people to worship God, our Maker and our Sustainer.
So do we recognize the source of our growth as children of God.

Invocation
Gracious and wise God, we thank you for Sabbath rest. In your wisdom you recognize that we, your children, need time off from the hectic schedule of daily living, time to focus on those things that are of ultimate meaning and worth: our relationship with you and those bonds of love that link us to family. Moreover, we need the rest, that we be restored in body, mind, and spirit. For only so will we be prepared, not merely to endure, but to respond creatively to the challenges of this week and every week. Thus do we seek your presence and guidance in worship — the encouragement of your Word and the refreshing of your Spirit. We pray in the name of the Lord of the Sabbath, the name of Jesus the Christ. Amen.

Call to Confession
Even as many a Jew in Jesus' day squeezed joy out of the Sabbath, so are we in our day guilty of stripping holiness from the Sabbath. In our society it seems that anything goes on this day. Far from

being a day to honor God, and so find ourselves refreshed spiritually, it has become a day to pursue one's own personal pleasure. Instead of building up the total person with such resources of renewal as God can offer, we continue to push ourselves to the brink of emptiness, of estrangement from that which ultimately counts and makes for life, in other words, to the very point of spiritual exhaustion. Let us in confession ask forgiveness and a sure word from God regarding our future.

Prayer of Confession
God of all wisdom, God of all love, God of Sabbath rest and renewal, we think that we can go and go and go and never have our spiritual tanks run dry. Whereas we value a good night's sleep for the refreshing of our physical body, we skimp on the time allocated for spiritual renewal. Just think how fidgety we become when the worship hour is extended by just a few minutes. The thought of a whole day, a Sabbath devoted to prayer and praise, a day wherein all members of the family seek to honor you and together to grow in your way, why that boggles the mind and strains to the limit our concept of the possible. Yet you rested, O God, and you would have us rest, that with renewed perspective and vigor we may be able faithfully to pursue the holy and so find purpose and joy in our living. Forgive us, we pray, past failures in this regard, and create in us a right spirit to truly remember the Sabbath day and keep it holy. With Christ as our guide, we would like to give it a try. Grant us another opportunity. Amen.

Words of Assurance
God is indeed merciful and gracious! When others in exasperation give up on us, God with patience awaits our about face and our return to the family. God's arms are ever open to embrace us and to receive us back — that we might rest in his presence, and so be revitalized for faithful witness and for useful service in the world around.
Thanks be to God — that rest and renewal are gifts of God ever available to us.

Psalter Reading (Psalm 121)
I lift up my eyes to the hills — from where will my help come?
My help comes from the Lord, who made heaven and earth.
He will not let your foot be moved; he who keeps you will not slumber.
He who keeps Israel will neither slumber nor sleep.
The Lord is your keeper; the Lord is your shade at your right hand.
The sun shall not strike you by day, nor the moon by night.
The Lord will keep you from all evil; he will keep your life.
The Lord will keep your going out and your coming in from this time on and forevermore.

Offering Sentences
Thanksgiving to God, concern for the well-being of friend and neighbor, our own desire to grow in spirit — all find tangible expression in the tithes and offerings that we now bring and dedicate to God's work in this place. May we all act from glad, grateful, and generous hearts, willing that God direct us in each gift's use.

Prayer of Dedication
Grant us the joy of participating in the use of these gifts, O God. In your wisdom, lead us to those places where healing is needed, where growth can be encouraged, where hope can be kindled, where love that is shared can truly make a difference. May a portion of this giving enable Sabbath rest and renewal; yet another portion, the fulfilling of your mission in the world. May all be done according to your will and to further your way. For so do we ask this in Jesus' name. Amen.

Benediction
May you find on every Sabbath day that nurturing, that empowering which will enable you to be a faithful witness and servant of God throughout the week. Utilize both the riches and the rest of the Sabbath to prepare you fully for that joyful task of being a child of the Most High, called to a very special place in God's creation, there to represent God. You have been called — and prepared — and now sent. Amen!

Saints

John 6:20-31

Call to Worship
In company with saints of all times and places, we too come to worship God.
For saints are those who, called by God, then trust in God.
The call is that we pursue relationships rather than possessions.
Such a focus to life, we know, runs counter to society's norm.
Yet here would God introduce us to life abundant, a life of certainty, security, and peace.
We come here to learn of this, and then to live it.
So are we invited to join the ranks of the saints.
So would we pursue the things of God, and allow them to mold us and direct us.

Invocation
God, your call is a strange one. You exalt the poor, those who hunger and thirst, those who are neglected, exploited, and excluded. What about those who are healthy and wealthy and wise? Why have you so turned the world upside down? Or, maybe it is *we* who have turned the world upside down. Though it makes little sense to us, obviously it makes sense to you. Yet those called saints every once in a while emerge, risk doing it your way, and so find your way to be true. Here in worship, O God, show us what you would have *us* do, and lead us to risk the doing. In the name of Jesus. Amen.

Call to Confession
We admire saints, yet most often we distance ourselves from them, for we feel that in no way can we match their dedication, their good deeds, their holiness. So do we sell ourselves short, and revert to a fearful, tame, and rather pathetic existence, taking few risks and providing little in the way of service to our neighbor — shrinking rather than growing. So do we miss the whole point of the kingdom's coming: that sharing by all will mean scarcity for

none. Do we dare confess this — and allow God entry into our lives to change them?

Prayer of Confession
Gracious God, the gospel indeed appears a topsy-turvy thing to us, for what we would call success you term failure. Rather than seek to position ourselves first, you tell us that we should instead place ourselves last. Those who are poor in spirit, those who humble themselves, are blessed, whereas blessing is withheld from the proud and the mighty. Rather than lord it over the one who has less, we are to empathize with this sister or brother, indeed come to that person's aid. Even as we say these things, so do we realize how far we are missing the mark. And missing the mark is sin. Forgive us, O God; show mercy upon our ignorance, upon our willful wrongdoing. But more than that, patiently guide us, we pray, into the right path, and inspire us to walk there. For so will we at last be following the way of the Christ, in whose name we are bold enough to pray. Amen.

Words of Assurance
God's call can still be heard in this place. It is the call to "Follow me" — in faithfulness to all, the greatest and the least, but especially mindful of the least. If this means turning the things of the world on their head, so be it. For God's love will show the world; God's love indeed will prevail. God includes each of us in that love; moreover, God would grant each of us the opportunity to minister that love.
Let us thank God by so ordering our lives to seize the opportunity.

Psalter Reading (from Psalm 16)
I say to the Lord, "You are my Lord; I have no good apart from you."
As for the saints in the land, they are the noble, in whom is all my delight.
The Lord is my chosen portion and my cup; you hold my lot.
The boundary lines have fallen for me in pleasant places, I have a goodly heritage.

I bless the Lord who gives me counsel; in the night also my heart instructs me.
I keep the Lord always before me; because he is at my right hand, I shall not be moved.
Therefore my heart is glad, and my soul rejoices; my body also rests secure.
For you do not give me up to Sheol, or let your faithful one see the Pit.
You show the way of life.
In your presence there is fullness of joy; in your right hand are pleasures evermore.

Offering Sentences
Saints of God do not hold back. Saints always offer — all that can be offered at a given moment. So is the love of God made available to those in need. So does the saint grow in understanding of what in truth is the essence of living. Let us give — as saints would give.

Prayer of Dedication
Though at times, Lord, we may feel anything but saintly, use us nonetheless, use us that your will be done in this small part of your creation. Since you value every part and consider none beyond the bounds of your love, use *these* gifts, we pray, that they may indeed demonstrate the extent of that love for all people — the power of love to heal, and the wonder of love to unite those who before had been separate and ill at ease. This do we ask, those who would be your saints. Amen.

Benediction
God sends out saints into a topsy-turvy world. Are you one of them? By the grace of God, may it be so. And if so, know that Jesus walks with you. Amen!

Second Sunday Of Easter

Romans 10:14-18
John 20:19-31

Call to Worship
This is the second Sunday of Easter.
Easter is not confined to a day but reflects a new way of life.
We are to be an Easter people.
We are ones who proclaim and live the resurrection.
Let our worship today reflect the joy of knowing the risen Christ.
Let our faith boldly state what we have heard and seen and believe.

Invocation
O God, we are the people of a long and joyful heritage. From those who first saw the risen Lord to communities of believers today, we share the resurrection song of new life, new life made possible by holy love. Though today we do not see the resurrected Christ as did those first disciples, we nonetheless by faith know that he lives. There are signs all around us that point to this: lives transformed, lives that now risk themselves in love for Jesus. This is the message — good news of life abundant and eternal for all — broadcast far and wide, to heal lives and to give them a holy meaning and purpose. So, let *us* be part of that joyous entourage and carry with us wherever we go the label: Easter people. This, to herald your Son's name. Amen.

Call to Confession
Why would anyone *not* want to walk wholeheartedly in the way of the risen Christ? It is the way of life, the way of joy and hope and fulfillment. Why be at all hesitant, or withhold a part of self? Each of us will answer in his or her own way, as we examine the response we give to the call of Christ. From each of us will come forth words of confession, as we sadly but truthfully acknowledge that we have yet to reach that complete and full commitment to our God.

Prayer of Confession

Gracious and eternal God, you set before us the way of life. It is the way that leads through death to resurrection, a way that fulfills the meaning and purpose of life as you intend it to be. Help us, we pray, that we be willing to allow certain incomplete and unwholesome parts of ourselves to die, that the Spirit of the living Christ might gift us with new beginnings and set us on paths that spell freedom, growth, and service in your name. Moreover, at the same time, may doubt, fear, and uncertainty die, as we more and more become convinced of the power of holy love, a love meant for each of us, a love that can transform that which is selfish and worn into a brilliance of being that is all-giving and ever-lasting. May we gladly reach out to receive, even as you, God, are so eager to give — that Easter take root and blossom in this place. In Christ's name. Amen.

Words of Assurance

God is light; in God there is no darkness at all. If we choose to walk in this light, that which is incomplete, imperfect, and impure will be removed from our lives, this by virtue of Christ's great gift of life to us. So will we find ourselves able to follow in the steps of our Lord. Christ has prepared the way to life abundant and eternal. It is now for us to accept the gift — with gladness of heart and humbleness of spirit.
Praise be to God who loves us so, who through Christ would have us live.

Psalter Reading (from Psalm 118)

I shall not die, but I shall live, and recount the deeds of the Lord.
I thank you that you have answered me and have become my salvation.
The stone that the builders rejected has become the chief cornerstone.
This is the Lord's doing; it is marvelous in our eyes.
This is the day that the Lord has made; let us rejoice and be glad in it.
The Lord is God, and he has given us light.

You are my God, and I will give thanks to you; you are my God, I will extol you.
O give thanks to the Lord, for he is good, for his steadfast love endures forever.

Offering Sentences
It is with thanksgiving that we respond to the goodness of our God. Thanksgiving, we find, can take many a tangible form and expression, such as the tithes and offerings we now bring forward, this to further the work of Christ's church in this place, indeed the work of Christ's church in many places round the world. Let our gifts be the glad response of an Easter people, those who know what it means to live by the power of the resurrection.

Prayer of Dedication
There are many who have not heard. There are many who have heard but have yet to believe. There are many who believe yet need to be supported in their infant faith, that they might grow to a greater depth of maturity. In each case, we have a responsibility and a mission. Thus do we pray: Holy God, by your Spirit's leading, may these tithes and offerings be directed to those arenas of service where they can make a profound difference in the lives of individuals, in the life of community, and in the fulfilling of your reconciling purpose for the whole of creation. This, that the name of Christ be praised. Amen.

Benediction
"Blessed are those who have not seen and yet have come to believe." So would the power of God sustain us in our faith. If we but allow it, God promises to enrich our lives beyond measure. Yield, I implore you, to the prompting of a loving God.

A Servant Cleansing

John 13:1-9
Matthew 27:15-26

Call to Worship
Though he was in the form of God ...
He took the form of a servant.
And being found in human form ...
He humbled himself.
He became obedient to the point of death ...
Yes, even death on a cross.
So at the name of Jesus do we bend our knee ...
And does our tongue confess that Jesus Christ is Lord.

Invocation
How strange that you, O God, should come to us as a servant. In that guise we might very well overlook you. Yet by identifying with us and with our needs, we know that you care. For yours is not an intimidating presence but rather an encouraging one, one that sets for us the good example. We pray that we might see you clearly during this hour of worship; and having seen, then be prepared to follow. That will mean a servant posture for us too, yet one laden with purpose and true joy. In this meek and humble way, guide us, Lord, for then we shall be whole. In your name do we ask it. Amen.

Call to Confession
Too often do we rely on our resources alone to cleanse and to make us whole. When will we learn that we cannot cleanse ourselves of impurity? However, standing close at hand is the one who says, "I can cleanse, refresh, and restore you." What will it take — that we believe this? First, a *confession* of our spiritual condition, and then the *desire* with all of one's heart to seek a better way. Let all who are thus minded join with me as we open our lives to God in prayer, asking that we be cleansed, filled, and directed.

Prayer of Confession
We too, God, must say with the prophet Isaiah of old, "I am a person of unclean lips, and I live among a people of unclean lips." Though I like to think that I can turn around and follow you whenever I wish, habits, patterns, and routines inevitably lock me into that old unprofitable course which leads me further and further from your way. The good I would do, I must confess I do not do. And though I say that discipleship is for me, I cannot even set myself on the right road, let alone walk down it faithfully. I am finally brought to that point of asking your help, O God. I do mean it! In truth, we all mean it! We need to be cleansed and led aright, and only you can do it. Your love alone has the presence, the power, the persistence. We ask, we humbly ask, for that love and the restoration of wholeness that it can bring. We ask this in the name of Jesus, who proclaimed your love, and in sharing it, lived it fully. Amen.

Words of Assurance
Hear the voice of Jesus say, "Let me cleanse you, refresh you, restore you. You need only ask with a contrite heart and you will receive." Let us rejoice in a God who deals so graciously with us. We are indeed forgiven, and renewed life in Christ is ours today.
Glory to God that God's love so provides life for us all.

Psalter Reading (from Psalm 51)
Have mercy on me, O God, according to your steadfast love; according to your abundant mercy blot out my transgressions.
Wash me thoroughly from my iniquity, and cleanse me from my sin.
For I know my transgressions; and my sin is ever before me.
Against you, you alone, have I sinned, and done what is evil in your sight, so that you are justified in your sentence and blameless when you pass judgment.
Indeed, I was born guilty, a sinner when my mother conceived me.
You desire truth in the inward being; therefore teach me wisdom in my secret heart.

Purge me with hyssop, and I shall be clean; wash me, and I shall be whiter than snow.
Let me hear joy and gladness; let the bones that you have crushed rejoice.
Hide your face from my sins, and blot out all my iniquities.
Create in me a clean heart, O God, and put a new and right spirit within me.

Offering Sentences
The servant Christ demonstrates for us the correct posture for our giving. We are to kneel before our neighbors' needs and not be content until we have emptied ourselves in a love-inspired effort to fill them. We must learn to say with the Christ: none for self, and all for thee. Let our giving today come from such a posture.

Prayer of Dedication
Gifts blessed and directed by your Holy Spirit, O God, can transform the downcast, give hope to the discouraged, bring meaning and purpose to those who despair. So can the needy be converted — into persons fired by a heavenly zeal and touched by hope in the holy. May our gifts so be charged by your Spirit that they accomplish all of these wonders, and so make life a joy for many a soul around us. Prepare us for daily service, this with Christ as our Guide. Amen.

Benediction
Having been cleansed, having been fed at the table of our Lord, having been commissioned a servant of Jesus Christ, let us go forth to bring hope and healing to those around us, this by showing Christ to others in our living. Amen.

Sharing

Luke 16:19-31
1 Timothy 6:6-11, 17-19

Call to Worship
As we gather, we acknowledge that we have indeed been blessed.
It is true that God's good gifts surround us in abundance.
These gifts flow into our lives each day.
Our task is to let them flow through us to others.
As we open ourselves to God's Word and Spirit, this readily happens.
Let it happen this hour, as we come before God with hearts and minds ready to receive and to give.

Invocation
God, we thank you for healing and hope, for that peace which is both within and without, for life in all its abundance and fullness. All are the workings of your love, your power for good flowing from your holy presence to us and through us to others. This comes not in spurts or spasms, but is constantly being revealed and is placed each day at our disposal. Why? Because of who you are, O God; you would not do otherwise. You are faithful to your promises and to your being. We, loving Father, would learn that lesson of faithfulness. Thus, help us, we pray, in our worship, not only to be open to receive, but also open to give — that even as we receive blessing, we would be ready to bestow blessing, and this with great constancy, with a faith that wavers not but is daily being renewed. In your holy name, in the name of Jesus, do we pray that this will indeed be so. Amen.

Call to Confession
Life suggests flow rather than stagnation. The gifts of God are to flow; they are to be passed on — shared — given from the one to the other. How frequently, however, does sin clog the flow, and thus life ends in tragedy rather than joy. In those instances, blessings *to* a person never become blessings *through* that person to another. As we view our lives in this light, we must confess our

own shortcomings and ask for God's mercy — that with God's help the flow once again be restored. Let us approach God in prayer — that in the right spirit we be both bold enough and humble enough to ask this.

Prayer of Confession
Holy and compassionate God, God both just and loving, so much of our praying finds us asking — asking that we receive from your hand good gifts to so enrich our living. And you *have* so blessed us, time and time again. None of us can say that you have been less than completely faithful. Would that we could say the same about our gift-giving. For we admit that on numerous occasions we have denied our neighbor, we have denied both friend and stranger that love needed to mend and make the person whole. We've done this by failing to share the gifts that you have so liberally bestowed upon us. Lines of life get clogged because of our selfishness. Forgive us, Lord; rid us of this self-centeredness that so blights our living. Keep us from being that place where your blessings stagnate. Rather, teach us to share, to discover that joy in life is measured by being an instrument of blessing, instead of being a mere container of blessing. In this we would have Jesus show us the way. We ask that this be so. Amen.

Words of Assurance
God's blessings still come. They are rich and full and life-giving. God does not withhold them from us but instead says, "Come, and sample, and enjoy. Fill yourself, and then go and fill others. For you will enjoy these blessings even more by sharing them with others." You see, God still counts on us to be instruments of the holy, coming indeed to know the holy through the giving of gifts. Would we in any way betray such faithfulness and love?
No, not betray, but serve faithfully the God who places such confidence in us.

Psalter Reading (from Psalm 146)
Praise the Lord! Praise the Lord, O my soul!
I will praise the Lord as long as I live; I will sing praises to my God all my life long.

Happy are those whose help is the God of Jacob, whose hope is in the Lord their God,
Who made heaven and earth, the sea and all that is in them;
Who keeps faith forever; who executes justice for the oppressed; who gives food to the hungry.
The Lord sets the prisoners free; the Lord opens the eyes of the blind.
The Lord lifts up those who are bowed down, the Lord loves the righteous.
The Lord watches over the strangers; he upholds the orphan and the widow, but the way of the wicked he brings to ruin.
The Lord will reign forever, your God, O Zion, for all generations.
Praise the Lord!

Offering Sentences
Let us begin now — by allowing gifts of God to flow through us to sisters and brothers in need. Certainly there are many needs to be addressed in the present-day world around us, and we have many gifts of God to share. Let love be expressed in what we do here today. So do we present tithes and offerings — for God's work of healing and making whole.

Prayer of Dedication
May streams of living water flow forth from this congregation, O God. May we be known as a people who respond in love by giving *ourselves* — for the well-being of neighbor and thus to your service, Lord. Help us to mature in our faith by learning how much is enough for self, for this will mean that all of the rest can be shared to build up the neighbor and the neighborhood in love. So would we walk in the way of Jesus. Amen.

Benediction
Count your blessings and then share those blessings. So will you discover God's affirmation of life in all its fullness. Let the flow not only be *to* but *through*. Amen!

Shepherd

John 10:11-18

Call to Worship
We trust God to lead us, for the path through life at times seems unsure.
Like a good shepherd tending his flock, so does God lead us.
We trust that God will care for us, for our strength at times proves inadequate.
Like a good shepherd tending his flock, so does God care for us.
We trust God to protect us, for forces of evil and apathy surround us.
Like a good shepherd tending his flock, so does God keep us safe from harm.

Invocation
How *comforting* it is, O God, to realize that our needs are known; moreover, that it is your will that these needs be met with an abundance of good gifts. We praise you for this goodness, proof indeed of your shepherding love. How *encouraging* it is, O God, that we can face the day without fear, for then we can make use of the talents we have received, employing them gladly for another's good. We praise you for so enabling us to risk ourselves and yet feel secure. This too reflects in powerful fashion your shepherding love. How *confirming of faith* it is, O God, to discover that your ways will be the same tomorrow as they are today, for this knowledge then becomes a source of confidence and hope. We praise you for giving us a future ever supported by life-giving love. So will we be shepherded today and always. Hallelujah and amen!

Call to Confession
It is when we turn away from the Good Shepherd, whether this be through ignorance, pride, or foolishness, that we bring trouble, uncertainty, and grief upon ourselves. We expose ourselves to all of those forces around us that would undo us, this without the

armor of faith and love that God would provide. In retrospect, it seems an awful bargain, yet how often it is that we stray. Let us confess this, even as we seek to return.

Prayer of Confession
God, it is truly that strange side of us which insists that we can do it on our own. Yet how often we are willing to focus life, our own living, in that way. We look away from the good that you would offer, that guidance, that care which you so readily make available. We glibly announce to others that we will do it our own way, thank you. We spurn the assistance of those whose sole motive is love, preferring instead to stew in our own juice. For time will show that the path taken without you, O God, and without your love, is a forlorn path indeed. For we need those resources of inner strength, hope, and peace which you alone can provide, which you route to us if we would but be faithful servants. That remarkably can happen yet, as we learn to depend wholly upon you, as we acknowledge you to be the Good Shepherd of our lives. May each of us boldly make that affirmation of faith. Amen.

Words of Assurance
"In this is love, not that we loved God, but that God loved us and sent his Son to be the atoning sacrifice for our sins." God's motives are plain; they are born of forgiveness and love. Let us rejoice that the God who made us would so redeem us; and let us accept this good and amazing gift with gratitude.
Thanks be to God for a love so caring, so healing — one that guides us home.

Psalter Reading (Psalm 23)
The Lord is my shepherd, I shall not want.
He makes me lie down in green pastures;
He leads me beside still waters; he restores my soul.
He leads me in the paths of righteousness for his name's sake.
Even though I walk through the valley of the shadow of death, I fear no evil, for you are with me;
Your rod and your staff they comfort me.

You prepare a table before me in the presence of my enemies;
You anoint my head with oil; my cup runs over.
Surely goodness and mercy shall follow me all the days of my life,
And I shall dwell in the house of the Lord forever.

Offering Sentences
Compared to the gift of a life, how can anything we give possibly measure up? Perhaps it is not a matter of measuring up. Perhaps it is more a matter of gratitude, giving what we can out of a glad thanksgiving, this that others too may come to know God's good news, which is life for all. Let our giving be in this spirit.

Prayer of Dedication
Gracious God, Jesus spoke of "other sheep who do not belong to this fold," affirming that it was his intent to include them too. *We* are part of that other fold, and so are still others. May what we offer here be used by your Spirit to awaken more and more to the wonder of your love and care — that their lives be changed here on earth and for all eternity. May our deeds likewise reflect a faithfulness to your word and holy purpose. In Jesus' name. Amen.

Benediction
Depart from this place knowing that God will be by your side during all of the coming week — guiding, supporting, challenging, and calming you. So does the Good Shepherd care for his sheep. Go, thus, in peace. Be it unto you according to your faith.

Songs Of The Season/Advent

Luke 1:39-56
Micah 5:2-5a

Call to Worship
We come ready to receive what God shall give.
We come with a willingness to be used in the service of our God.
We would be counted among those who are poor in spirit.
For those are the ones who recognize their spiritual needs and gladly are dependent upon God to meet those needs.
Thus in worship, with face turned toward God, do we implore God's goodness.
In worship, with heart turned toward God, we have faith that God will use even us to enact a divine work here on earth.

Invocation
Lord God of mercy, purpose, and power, it is with a divine purpose that you invest humble vessels with power. Your purpose is mercy and your power that of a compassionate heart, a heart which willingly shares its abundance with others. As we consider here in worship what it means to serve you, may life's real values impress us too: those of patience and humility, gentleness and compassion, and love. May these prompt us to a service that seeks to reflect in daily living a way of life faithful to you and of meaning to those around us. O God, we begin our worship with this prayer of praise and petition offered in Jesus' name. Amen.

Call to Confession
We as a church must learn to measure our wealth not by the size of our endowments nor by the beauty of our buildings, but by the poor in body, mind, and spirit who find comfort and confidence in our presence. Insofar as we fall short of this, we fail in God's purpose for us. Let us then be honest to admit this shortcoming, this sin, ask forgiveness, and be ready to follow God's leading into a better, a more faithful and fruitful future.

Prayer of Confession

The treasures of the church, O God, are those persons in need whom we have served with life. How often, though, we define our treasure in other terms, and so miss the joy of serving in your name. Give us the forthrightness of Elizabeth and the humility of Mary, we pray, that we be fit instruments, which you can then mold to your purpose. For unless we become your caring presence to those around us, we shall remain but a hollow shell of that which we could be, a noisy gong, a clanging cymbal. Rather, we implore that you fill us with your love. May we readily, eagerly accept it, and then use it by sharing it, for so will we discover that in the sharing of this, your most precious gift, it will remain available to us in never-ending supply. Such is the message and the example of Jesus the Christ, in whose name we pray. Amen.

Words of Assurance

Hear the words of the Christ, "Whoever wishes to be great among you must be your servant, and whoever wishes to be first must be slave of all. For the Son of man came not to be served but to serve...." Jesus gave us in his own life the example. Let us each one follow that example and know the joy of discipleship.
Thanks be to God for so loving the world — and us — that we are led to life, life that is true and lasting in his name.

Psalter Reading (from Psalm 145)

The Lord is gracious and merciful, slow to anger and abounding in steadfast love.
The Lord is good to all, and his compassion is over all that he has made.
The Lord is faithful in all his words, and gracious in all his deeds.
The Lord upholds all who are falling, and raises up all who are bowed down.
The Lord is just in all his ways, and kind in all his doings.
The Lord is near to all who call on him, to all who call on him in truth.
He fulfills the desire of all who revere him; he also hears their cry, and saves them.

The Lord watches over all who love him ... So will my mouth speak the praise of the Lord, and all flesh will bless his holy name forever and ever.

Offering Sentences
The frenzy of this buying season is almost over. The gifts have been purchased and wrapped. How many of them, we might ask, are for the poor, the poor in body, mind, and spirit? What will you be giving them this season, that Christ's message of love be made known to them? For in this manner will you be welcoming the Christ into your heart and life. Let us so receive the tithes and the offerings of this Lord's Day.

Prayer of Dedication
Gifts that are truly love have the ability to reach into the deepest, darkest corners and so bring light where before there had only been darkness or at best dimness of purpose. May these our gifts, brought now into the presence of the Holy, author such miracles of love and life — that darkness flee and that the light of that holy night so long ago be experienced anew in the hearts of many. With you, O Lord, this can happen. We pray that it be so. Amen.

Benediction
Christmas comes anew! Let us sing, "Noel!" In humbleness of spirit and with the joy of Christ in our hearts, let us ready ourselves to celebrate once again the coming of our God, our God who comes to live in the midst of us. Hallelujah! He comes! Amen!

Spirit Of Truth

John 14:8-17, 25-27
Romans 8:14-17

Call to Worship
Come, Holy Spirit, come!
Come with wind and fire!
Be that Counselor that we sorely need for our living.
Be that Spirit of Truth that will lead us to correct understandings.
Let us here in worship sense the enthusiasm that you bring into our midst.
May your presence and power further transform us into dedicated children of God.

Invocation
God, you who are both Spirit and Holy, we welcome you as you make your lively presence known among us. How amazing that you consider us worthy of your attention, your concern, and your care. How we need understanding! Truth so often eludes us. You would make it clearly known. Self-interest prompts so much of the counsel we receive. You would guide us, however, in ways that truly cause us to grow. We cower rather than with courage defend the truth. We fail to realize that you stand by our side to support us whenever the going gets rough. Let us this day, this hour of worship, sense afresh that your presence and power are ever with us; and in so doing, help us to be thankful. Amen.

Call to Confession
God is here — now — in all the fullness of God's strength and mercy. God's presence fills this sanctuary with joy and hope, peace and love. The wonder of it is that we can tap into this presence — that our lives too can be full of purpose and enthusiasm and gratefulness to the Giver. But do we? God with glad Spirit gives. How do we feel about receiving? Let our answer be a prayer of confession to the Holy.

Prayer of Confession

Your riches, O God, all the wonder, the magnificence of your presence and power, are here before us, offered to us, an amazing gift for our taking. If we dare admit our need, if we are courageous enough to acknowledge our dependence, then we shall be eager to accept with love those resources given out of love. For you would make us a whole, a complete people of God. Why then are we so stubborn — to receive that which is good, whose purpose is our salvation? Forgive us all of our meager attempts still to do it on our own. Let both wind and flame of your presence purge us of all selfish leanings, all prideful thoughts and actions — that we open ourselves fully to the guidance of your holy will. For that will be joy to us, hope for our neighbor, and peace for us all. This we ask in Jesus' name, who indeed has fulfilled his promise that the Holy Spirit would come and rest upon us all. Amen.

Words of Assurance

Jesus would have us affirm that in every way God works for our well-being. Yet another manifestation of this is the coming of God's Spirit, God's presence and power among us. This too is for our good — that all of us who comprise the family of God be one in spirit, one in heart, mind, and purpose. This being so, we can be enthusiastic about our future, for God is here to guide us into it. **We turn our lives over to God's leading, that by the work of the Holy Spirit in us and among us God's will be done. Praise be to God, for this is God's gift of life to us all.**

Psalter Reading (from Psalm 104)

O Lord, how manifold are your works!
In wisdom you have made them all; the earth is full of your creatures.
Yonder is the sea, great and wide, creeping things innumerable are there, living things both small and great.
There go the ships, and leviathan that you formed to sport in it.
These all look to you to give them their food in due season.
When you give to them, they gather it up; when you open your hand, they are filled with good things.

When you hide your face, they are dismayed; when you take away their breath they die and return to their dust.
When you send forth your spirit, they are created; and you renew the face of the ground.
May the glory of the Lord endure forever; may the Lord rejoice in his works —
Who looks on the earth and it trembles, who touches the mountains and they smoke.
I will sing to the Lord as long as I live; I will sing praise to my God while I have being;
May my meditation be pleasing to him for I rejoice in the Lord.

Offering Sentences

God provides the gifts. It is up to us to pass them on — that all in God's creation may be alive with hope and eager to participate in the daily blessings of life. What will we pass on this morning? May what we now give faithfully represent God's bounty to us and our joy in being able to serve another in God's name. Let us present tithes and offerings out of fullness of hearts blessed many times over by God's love.

Prayer of Dedication

May the wonder of your love, O God, the wonder of your Spirit's presence and power, be expressed in these gifts that we humbly yet joyously dedicate to your continuing work of making all peoples one. Let gifts be matched by actions, actions that through this week will reveal your reconciling presence and your healing power in our many walks of life. For so would we be faithful to your leading in our lives. Gladly do we promise all, in Jesus' name. Amen.

Benediction

Let the Spirit of God, the Spirit of Truth, guide you in your walk through life this week. Allow the Spirit to support you when truth is challenged and your own strength falters. Indeed, permit the Spirit to open to you a greater understanding of truth. Moreover, accompany the Spirit, as God leads you to further sites of service. So will your life be full, charged with joy and fraught with meaning. Amen!

Spiritual Gifts/One Body

1 Corinthians 12:1-11
John 2:1-11

Call to Worship
We come here as people of many talents;
Yet we confess a common faith in one Creator and in one Savior Jesus Christ.
We gather as a particular expression of the church of Jesus Christ;
Yet we affirm the church universal and all in Christ as our sisters and brothers.
In each case, we would discover how individual members fit into the whole —
That our witness be whole — that the world may see and believe.

Invocation
We praise your love, O God, which can indeed make all things whole. For this love of yours is at all times found to be working miracles in our midst. You work them through a whole host of instruments, all attuned to your will and purpose. Help us to appreciate these many and varied manifestations of your power and tender care. May we joyfully affirm them all and be ready to work in concert with each, thereby acknowledging that wonderful tapestry wherein all are woven into one great offering of life and peace and beauty — this for the healing of the nations, this to display your glory in all the world. Praise to you, O God, that wherever there be estrangement and division, you are present to reconcile and unite. Amen.

Call to Confession
How appreciative are we of the spiritual gifts of other brothers and sisters in Christ? How many Christians of other congregations do we even know? With how many do we labor side by side in ministries of hope and healing? Could it be that even within our

own ranks there is estrangement and division, not so apparent perhaps, but nonetheless there and deadly? Let us look at our own witness to the oneness of the body of Christ, and let us confess wherein we have failed to live as one.

Prayer of Confession

Though we would like to think that we are all one in Christ — in our own congregation, in Christian witness within our community, in holding high the banner of Christ the world around — yet we fail in so many ways to be in communion with sisters and brothers in Christ — at all these levels and locales. We confess our ignorance of our brother's need. We confess our ignorance of our sister's hurt. We confess our apathy in that we allow this ignorance to persist, that we see not the urgency of repairing the many breeches that cause the body of Christ to be broken and for that very reason ineffective. Awaken us again to our calling as your church, O God. Forgive us these shortcomings that have ended in division, and enable us to value that unity of spirit which can again make us healthy. Restore us, we pray, in the name of our Savior Christ. Amen.

Words of Assurance

In spite of our waywardness, Christ bestows love, forgives, and offers to make us whole. In spite of our stubborn individualism, Christ grants communion about one table and an appreciation of each sister and brother. In spite of our many loose ends, Christ can nonetheless make of them a single weaving of great beauty and usefulness.
Praise God for this, which is miracle indeed.

Psalter Reading (from Psalm 36)

Your steadfast love, O Lord, extends to the heavens, your faithfulness to the clouds.
Your righteousness is like the mighty mountains, your judgments are like the great deep; you save humans and animals alike.

How precious is your steadfast love, O God! All people may take refuge in the shadow of your wings.
They feast on the abundance of your house, and you give them drink from the river of your delights.
For with you is the fountain of life; in your light we see light.
O continue your steadfast love to those who know you, and your salvation to the upright of heart!

Offering Sentences
Do you believe in your inmost being that God has the power to turn your offering into a miracle, a miracle that will benefit a whole host of God's people in need? Let your faith grow, even as you allow your offering of self to grow — and you will be amazed at what God can do and will do through you. Let us as an act of thanksgiving, and with great joy, present our tithes and offerings for God's work here on this earth.

Prayer of Dedication
Even as we entrust these tithes and offerings to your holy work, O God, so do we entrust the living of our lives to your service. May we with enthusiasm and diligence seek to work with other Christians, this in a spirit of unity and peace, that all of those around may see the genuineness of love and compassion that we share, and will so be led also to place their faith in you. It is to your work of reconciling and uniting that we give our complete devotion. In Jesus' name. Amen.

Benediction
Open your eyes and your heart that you may see the miracles that God is performing all around you. And may one of those miracles be Christians laboring side by side with one another in complete harmony, devotion, and unity. For so do *we* proclaim God's power and goodness. So be it! Amen!

Stewardship

Matthew 25:14-30
2 Corinthians 9:5-15

Call to Worship
We have indeed been blessed by God.
And God calls forth from us both thanksgiving and accountability.
To be faithful to God, we must take risks for God.
Yes, as stewards we are to use wisely all that God has entrusted to us.
We seek to do this in ways that are both compassionate and just.
For where one is in need, there are we to be found sharing the gifts of God.
Let us learn more about this as we worship —
This to prepare us for the living of our daily lives.

Invocation
God, in your presence there is always abundance. This you share with us, even as you call us to be stewards of these riches. Indeed, we experience a myriad of opportunities in this life to be faithful to that call; and so do we find ourselves shouldering many a responsibility. To be faithful and diligent, we need both wisdom and zeal. Thus, in worship would we hear your Word and be open to the leading of your Spirit. For without your constant encouragement we too easily revert to self-centered ways. Even as you are near us at all times, we pray that this hour may bring a special sense of your presence, this through Christ, as real and relevant. In his name do we pray. Amen.

Call to Confession
Our intentions are often quite honorable. Our actions, however, tell a far different story. For we too readily claim things to be "ours," rather than acknowledge ownership as God's. We view blessings as deserved rather than confess them to be the gifts of God they are. In these ways do we miss the mark. Let us admit this and name it sin.

Prayer of Confession
How trusting you are of us, O God, to call us stewards. Would that we be as trusting, as we seek to use resources wisely in daily living — both for your glory and for the world's well-being. We confess that this steward role does not come easily to us. We would much rather be owner and sole proprietor. So do we try to usurp your role, O God, and in this way edge you out of the picture — and out of our lives. That can lead to but one end: bankruptcy. No wonder our lives then become lackluster, without direction, void of meaningful relationships. We need to change, change the focus back to a faithful stewardship. On our own, though, we know that we shall never be able to do this. Thus, not only do we ask forgiveness for past unfaithfulness, but guidance and a measure of strength to follow your way for us. In humbleness, yet with resolve, do we seek this as we bring these petitions before your throne of grace. Amen.

Words of Assurance
God is always present, enabling us to realize the best possible return on our investment. And this we shall do, if we entrust ourselves completely to his leading. An unproductive past is left behind; great potential, we find, is there to be realized — all because God's love can redeem our failure, and yet engage us in creative stewardship. An indescribable gift, yes, this love of God, made known to us fully in the ministry, death, and resurrection of Jesus Christ.
Let us accept the gift and be faithful to the calling made anew to us in Christ.

Psalter Reading (from Psalm 116)
Gracious is the Lord, and righteous; our God is merciful.
The Lord protects the simple; when I was brought low, he saved me.
Return, O my soul, to your rest, for the Lord has dealt bountifully with you.
For you have delivered my soul from death, my eyes from tears, my feet from stumbling.

I walk before the Lord in the land of the living.
I have kept my faith, even when I said, "I am greatly afflicted."
What shall I return to the Lord for all his bounty to me?
I will lift up the cup of salvation and call on the name of the Lord.
I will pay my vows to the Lord in the presence of all his people.
Precious in the sight of the Lord is the death of his faithful ones.
O Lord, I am your servant ... You have loosed my bonds.
I will offer to you a thanksgiving sacrifice and call on the name of the Lord.
I will pay my vows to the Lord in the presence of all his people,
In the courts of the house of the Lord, in your midst, O Jerusalem. Praise the Lord.

Offering Sentences
What is the bottom line for us? What purpose have we, really, in our giving? A cheerful expression of thanksgiving, *or* a necessary but uninspiring duty? A spontaneous reaching out to another in love, *or* an obligation prompted and then reluctantly presented? A first fruit, the result of blessing, *or* a leftover, the result of prior selfishness? You answer these questions each week as you present gifts to God — for God's work. How will you answer today?

Prayer of Dedication
It is truly amazing, O God, how you take our little and magnify it into much. Such is the work of holy love, as it transforms gift and makes it blessing. We would ask that you do that with the gifts that we here present — that they enable the ill to become well, the weak to become strong, the troubled to become sure, the fearful to become hopeful. Use us, we pray, that we daily bring such blessing into the lives of those around us. All exemplifying your love, and offered in the name of Christ. Amen.

Benediction
May all of us find joy in investing God's way, so using love to transform gifts into blessings. For then the bottom line shall be abundant life for all. And so shall we receive the words, "Well done, good and faithful servant." Go forth from here now and live this! Amen!

Storms

Matthew 14:22-33

Call to Worship
We worship God, whose creation is good.
Storms in life, therefore, must have a purpose.
We worship God, who is in control, whose will is supreme.
Even storms must bend to this will and so be used by God.
We worship God, whose love makes things whole.
Thus do fears subside and healthy expectations of life arise.
So do we come to worship, expecting good from God.
And we shall not be disappointed, for so will God gift us.

Invocation
God, we know that storms do arise. Life, at times, can be quite tempestuous. Yet you are ever present — to still storms both within and without. May we have the courage — and the good sense — to admit our need and to welcome your intervention. For you would use even that which seems the greatest threat, that through it we might grow in understanding, in resolve, and in strength to persevere and overcome. May we here in worship discover more fully your way with us — such that even in the midst of that which challenges us sorely, we may find peace for our souls and confidence for our living. We pray in the name of Jesus, the one who can truly accomplish this in us. Amen.

Call to Confession
It is our greed, our pride, and our fear that defeat us, a focus upon self rather than upon God. Either we think that we can manage on our own, or we despair of any solution. So often in all of this there seems to be no room for God, let alone the welcoming of God as first in our lives. Let us confess how *we* are the obstacle to our own well-being — and so make way for God's mercy and direction.

Prayer of Confession

When storm winds blow — in our lives and in the life of the world around — where can we turn, O God of power and purpose, except to you? Our lives flounder; we grow discouraged. Yet you have the power to still the storm, to bring peace to our living. Then why is it that we so often ignore these gracious overtures, the gifts of acceptance, love, and guidance that you offer? All are here — and available — for our well-being. Help us to overcome doubt with faith, a centering on self with a giving of self, a compulsion to control with a yielding of spirit — that we be led from death to a life unimaginably rich and full. For you would introduce us, Lord, to abundant living, fullness of joy, and a power that can truly accomplish marvelous things in your name. May that happen to each of us. Give us the courage to allow it to happen. In Jesus' name. Amen.

Words of Assurance

With Isaiah the prophet let us too say, "Surely God is my salvation; I will trust, and will not be afraid, for the Lord God is my strength and my might; he has become my salvation." Let us too trust, for God bestows mercy, a saving grace that stills the storm, and so prepares us for service in his name.
Thanks be to God for renewed hope and a confidence that is born of love.

Psalter Reading (from Psalm 65)

Praise is due to you, O God, in Zion; and to you shall vows be performed.
O you who answer prayer, to you all flesh shall come.
When deeds of iniquity overwhelm us, you forgive our transgressions.
Happy are those whom you choose and bring near to live in your courts. We shall be satisfied with the goodness of your house, your holy temple.
By awesome deeds you answer us with deliverance, O God of our salvation; you are the hope of all the ends of the earth and of the farthest seas.

By your strength you established the mountains; you are girded with might.
You silence the roaring of the seas, the roaring of the waves, the tumult of the peoples.
Those who live at earth's farthest bounds are awed by your signs; you make the gateways of the morning and the evening shout for joy.

Offering Sentences
We are called upon to make sacrifices — of thanksgiving. In response to the many blessings of God, let our thanks be reflected in talents that are shared, in gifts that find use both near and far, and in time devoted to the well-being of others. Let ours be a joyful sacrifice, one that expresses a heartfelt thanks that we belong to the family of God.

Prayer of Dedication
Use these gifts, O God, to still storms, to bring encouragement, your calm and peace into lives that at present are distraught, yea even despairing, to spread your message of health and hope for body, mind, and spirit to many a needy soul both far away and near. Use these gifts — and us — to cause your way of love and peace to prosper here on this earth. In Christ's name we know that it can be so!

Benediction
We are sent forth from this place to be light, hope, and strength to others, that others may know that there is indeed a way through the storms of life to a safe haven and to a peace grounded in the assurance of God's love. May we forget ourselves long enough and thoroughly enough to be this kind of witness to our neighbor. Always and ever in Jesus' name. Amen.

Thanksgiving

Deuteronomy 26:1-11
John 6:25-35

Call to Worship
Thanksgiving — a day or an attitude?
Let it without fail be a part of our daily living,
Where thanks is given to God,
Where thanks is given to any who befriend us.
Let the people of God join together — to praise God for God's gifts of goodness.
We would have all around us know the source of the blessings we enjoy.

Invocation
God, we know that thanksgiving can never be feigned. It either comes from the heart, or clearly appears counterfeit. May our thanks to you, O God, always issue from the heart, and may each day bring forth its own particular expressions of gratitude and praise. May we remember as well that "Thank you," spoken often and genuinely, contributes in a significant way to the building of human relationships. Let no occasion where thanks is due escape our attention, but rather find us prepared to meet blessing with appreciation. So will each of us grow in our understanding of life, and will we as a body be faithfully the body of Christ. In his name do we pray. Amen.

A Litany of Thanks
For the first ray of light that announces the gift of a new day:
God of light, we thank you!
For the knowledge that in this new day we are not alone, but have the warmth of home and friends:
God of family and friends, we thank you!
For the benefit of community where we can feel both a sense of security and the confidence of belonging:
God of community and of communion, we thank you!

For the nourishment of body and spirit, which you provide abundantly:
God, you indeed provide for all our needs; we thank you!
For moments of solemn reflection and for times of laughter and good cheer:
God, you encourage us in all ways to grow; we thank you!
For beauty in nature and beauty in people:
God, you create all things beautiful and good; we thank you!
For the quiet of an evening and a day well spent; for the prospect of renewal and yet another day to come:
God of all of life, both the old and the new, we thank you! Amen.

Psalter Reading (Psalm 100)
Make a joyful noise to the Lord, all the earth.
Worship the Lord with gladness; come into his presence with singing.
Know that the Lord is God. It is he that made us, and we are his;
We are his people and the sheep of his pasture.
Enter his gates with thanksgiving, and his courts with praise.
Give thanks to him, bless his name.
For the Lord is good;
His steadfast love endures forever, and his faithfulness to all generations.

Offering Sentences
How do we *live* our thanksgiving? By faithfully following the example of our Savior, who thought not of selfish ambition and gain, but rather shared himself — all of his gifts and talents — with others, this as an expression of a continuous thanksgiving to God the Father. Such an offering was joyful, meaningful, and complete. Let us likewise render unto God the Father our thanksgiving, this through the offering of self that we bring forth and share.

Prayer of Dedication
Let this be, O God, our sacrifice of thanksgiving. May it serve to awaken others to your goodness — to mend that which is broken,

and to bring to full growth that which even now struggles for maturity. May our giving in every way reflect the thanksgiving which is the hallmark of a Christian. In Christ's name do we ask this. Amen.

Benediction
What will you feed others this Thanksgiving week? Hopefully food for the whole body. May it be that through you others will come to know the goodness of God, and will so join their words of thanksgiving with yours. Amen!

Things Of First Importance

Mark 12:28-34
Hosea 6:1-6

Call to Worship
The commandment above all others is that we love God with the whole of our being.
For this reason do we gather for worship — to make known our love for God.
Jesus added to this commandment another of equal importance: that we love our neighbor as our self.
Both in worship and in the world we would identify this neighbor and seek to make known a God-given love.
By having these as our priorities, we are not far from the kingdom of God.
Indeed, we would know God's rule in our lives — for this will be hope and joy and peace to us.

Invocation
God, both majestic and merciful, thank you for giving us a focus to our living. We truly know what is of first importance, that which would call forth from us the very best that we can offer. It centers in love for you and in service motivated by that love for the neighbor. Within the bounds of this love and service life finds its meaning. Help us in our worship, we pray, to keep this focus unimpaired — that we be wholehearted in our devotion and single-minded in our doing. In this way would we grow toward that maturity of spirit that you wish and would see in each of us. May it be so — as we hear your Word and follow in your Way. This, in Jesus' name. Amen.

Call to Confession
We tend to forget that living for God and neighbor in the world is of more importance than anything we do here in this church building. For great issues of love and justice far overshadow ritual and church housekeeping. It seems, though, that we continuously get

our cues mixed; and instead of playing in a major key, we play in a minor. Thus does Christ's mission suffer, does the neighbor's need go untended, and do we falter in our own growth as children of God. What will it take for us to recognize the true way and to walk in it? Let us come before God in prayer — to acknowledge, to implore, and in gratitude to receive.

Prayer of Confession

God of steadfast love, though we stray from those essentials that mark right living, you depart not from our side, but with great patience await our turning, that we follow again in the footsteps of our Lord. This means bowing before you; this means stooping to wash the feet of both neighbor and stranger. For only in this manner shall we be attuned to your Way and discover that which gives life both meaning and joy. So often do we get wrapped up in the demands of the day that we lose our focus; we see not the purpose that you have for our living. We find ourselves enmeshed in details and lose the larger vision. Help us to see our lives, individually and as family, as nothing apart from you, yet full of meaning and purpose as our actions imitate those of the Christ, as we live his way into the kingdom of God. Forgive us; direct us. We ask this, trusting in your love, which amazingly is always there and includes each and every one who would receive it. In Jesus' name. Amen.

Words of Assurance

Hear the words of the prophet Isaiah, words that announce the everlasting mercy of our God: "Seek the Lord while he may be found, call upon him while he is near; let the wicked forsake his way, and the unrighteous their thoughts; let them return to the Lord, that he may have mercy upon them, and to our God, for he will abundantly pardon." Know that these words are meant for you today, indeed for all who repent and believe.
Praise God that blessings for all of us still flow!

Psalter Reading (from Psalm 146)
Praise the Lord! Praise the Lord, O my soul!
I will praise the Lord as long as I live; I will sing praises to my God all my life long.
Do not put your trust in princes, in mortals, in whom there is no help.
When their breath departs, they return to the earth; on that very day their plans perish.
Happy are those whose help is the God of Jacob, whose hope is in the Lord their God,
Who made heaven and earth, the sea, and all that is in them;
Who keeps faith forever; who executes justice for the oppressed; who gives food to the hungry.
The Lord sets the prisoners free; the Lord opens the eyes of the blind.
The Lord lifts up those who are bowed down; the Lord loves the righteous.
The Lord watches over strangers; the Lord upholds the orphan and the widow, but the way of the wicked he brings to ruin.
The Lord will reign forever, your God, O Zion, for all generations.
Praise the Lord!

Offering Sentences
For God and for neighbor. How can we separate one from the other? In truth, we cannot. What we offer in love to our neighbor *is* our offering to God. Let our offering this day reflect how we define neighbor, and of equal importance, how we respond to that neighbor's need. For so will be our worship of God.

Prayer of Dedication
Our offerings join bread and wine on this holy table, O God. Just as we look upon the bread and the wine as consecrated elements, so would we consecrate the fruits of our labors to a holy purpose, that of making real your love to any and all in need. So use these gifts — that they convey your Way to the hearts of many. In Jesus' name. Amen.

Benediction
May each of us confess as did Jesus when asked which commandment is first of all: "You shall love the Lord your God with all your heart, and with all your soul, and with all your mind, and with all your strength." And may we too add as Jesus did: "And you shall love your neighbor as yourself." For those faithful to these commandments are indeed not far from the kingdom of God.

This Earthly Life

Deuteronomy 34:1-12
Romans 14:7-9

Call to Worship
On this earth, what is but one short life?
It is a gift from God.
And what are we to do with this life?
We are to give it back to God.
And how are we to do that?
We are to do that in worship and service.
Then let us look to God as we begin this worship.
We do this that we be equipped for service, our service that we render in God's name.

Invocation
O God, we spend but a short time on the face of this earth. We might say that we are only passing through. We want it to be right with you, yet we often find life around us to be extremely complex. Such a short time to do the right thing, with so many people and things pressing upon us, each calling upon us to act in this way or that. Yet you have set the way for us, the one true way, the way which indeed enables us to value that which is of utmost importance and then to use our time wisely to cultivate it and inculcate it in our living. All of this time with Jesus leading the way, in whose name we now pray. Amen.

Call to Confession
So often we take time, the little time at our disposal, for granted. We value things and people only after they are gone. Rather than returning God's gift of life by sharing it in love, we tend to hold onto it; we try in vain to hoard it, yet ultimately discover how truly empty our selfishness can be. Let us confess this in God's presence, asking pardon and the power for a full living of this day.

Prayer of Confession

We return, O God, to the desire within each of us that we want to be right with you. We confess, however, that we go about it in ways that negate this high aim and purpose in our living. For we are so concerned about making a name for ourselves that we fail to honor and praise your name. We are so engrossed in charting our own course that we fail to see how far we have strayed from the true course that you have set for our lives. We are seen to be wasting time, those valuable, those precious moments that can mean growth for us and health for the neighbor. All of us suffer because of this playing with life rather than truly living it. Help us to look upon all of life as your good gift. Pardon our past misuse of it; and guide us such that we value all of the days on this earth yet remaining to us. May we make them faithful reflectors of that which endures. So do we ask, O God, that your love redeem us and make us the whole people of God that you have created us to be. This in the name of our Redeemer Jesus the Christ, your Son, our hope of life this day and every day, forever and ever. Amen.

Words of Assurance

God desires not the death of a single lost sheep. Instead, God would have all find life and live that life abundantly. Such is the power of God's love that this can indeed happen, not in fantasy, but in fact. We will know that this is so even as we entrust ourselves into God's care and with determination and zeal follow the wondrous example that he has given us in Christ.
Praise be to God that by means of holy love we can truly live.

Psalter Reading (from Psalm 90)

Lord, you have been our dwelling place in all generations.
Before the mountains were brought forth, or ever you have formed the earth and the world, from everlasting to everlasting you are God.
You turn us back to dust, and say, "Turn back, you mortals."
For a thousand years in your sight are like yesterday when it is past, or like a watch in the night.

You sweep them away; they are like a dream, like grass that is renewed in the morning.
In the morning it flourishes and is renewed; in the evening it fades and withers.
These days of our life are seventy years, or perhaps eighty, if we are strong.
Even then their span is only toil and trouble; they are soon gone, and we fly away.
Let your work be manifest to your servants, and your glorious power to their children.
Let the favor of the Lord our God be upon us, and prosper for us the work of our hands — O prosper the work of our hands!

Offering Sentences

Gifts of gratitude take the form not only of funds donated for this good cause or that, but of time and talent, which can likewise be of great benefit to family, community, and world. The church is but one focus of giving, yet we of God's family hold it to be an important focus indeed, for here God's love can be clearly shown. As we now present for God's use today's gifts of gratitude, let us think of the many ways in which we can serve the church and its outreach in mission.

Prayer of Dedication

O bounteous Giver of all goodness, we too would give, and have the gift be good. For this to be so, help us, Lord, to give with the right spirit. Moreover, help us to give sacrificially, not because we must, but that our giving reflect a true devotion — our love for you and our love of neighbor. So let these in truth *be good* gifts, and with the assistance of your Holy Spirit, help us to direct them to those locales where they can promote healing, reconciliation, and peace. For so will we be announcing the reign of Christ on this earth. Amen.

Benediction

Whether we live or whether we die, we are the Lord's! What a magnificent affirmation of faith! Let it come from the lips of each one here present. For so would we undergird life with life. So can we be confident of this world's future — and *our* future. Let us then joyfully live, and radiate through all that we say and do this same message of joy and life to others.

Transfiguration/Fully Awake

Luke 9:28-36
Exodus 34:29-35

Call to Worship
We would be fully awake to the glory of God.
It is a wondrous presence that indeed invests all of creation.
Yet to witness it, we must in faith be willing to see.
Thus would worship focus on the holy, and so inspire us.
We use here the best of mind and spirit — our whole self —
That we be led to heightened perception and a deeper commitment.

Invocation
Gracious God, how wonderful that you grant us glimpses of the Holy, eyes that allow us to see if but for a moment the eternal. It is your expectation that by faith we receive these evidences of your power into our lives, that we discern your will, your purpose for each of us. You would thus have us appreciate life — life as we have been blessed to know it on earth, life as it is promised in your eternal realm so glorious as to be beyond our present comprehension and grasp. With life around us and before us, we pray that we be kept on the Way, your Way, O God, of grace and truth, in order that we grow into the full and complete children of the Holy that you mean us to be. Guide us this hour into a greater understanding and a deeper communion. This, in Jesus' name. Amen.

Call to Confession
Do we truly appreciate the Holy? Do we *see* the Holy — active in our lives and in the world around us? Indeed, what *is* real to us, that which governs our decisions, dictates our actions, determines our future? Are we fully awake to all that God would share with us? Each of us answers these questions in his or her own way. Let us, however, join voices in a common word of confession that includes us all.

Prayer of Confession
God, you are present, here, in our midst. You reveal your glory and majesty in many an insightful way to those with eyes to see and ears to hear. You would have us know your eternal purposes for humankind, indeed for the whole of your creation. Yet all too often we display a dullness, a spiritual stupor to things eternal — rather than be fully awake to receive your wisdom and power into our living. Love is always fully awake. We do not savor life to the full because, quite simply, love has not gained access to all aspects of our living. On certain occasions we prefer not to see, not to hear, not to be alert to your word of counsel, your gesture of mercy. In other words, not awake to love. So do we deprive ourselves of the life, life everlasting, life eternal, O God, that you offer us. We seek forgiveness and faith to be awake — that we might receive your life into our lives. That this happen and happen for all, Jesus opened the way. That way is still open today. With thanks to him do we pray. Amen.

Words of Assurance
How amazing that God persists, that life is still God's gift to us, that no force opposed to God and to life can endure, but will itself be transformed by the power of God's love, such that God be all in all, forever and ever. We know this to be true because of God's coming among us in Jesus Christ, who not only taught us, but by example, the example of his life-giving sacrifice, makes God's grace available to all.
We praise God's purpose, God's gift, God's everlasting love.

Psalter Reading (from Psalm 99)
The Lord is king; let the peoples tremble!
He sits enthroned upon the cherubim; let the earth quake!
The Lord is great in Zion; he is exalted over all the peoples.
Let them praise your great and awesome name. Holy is he!
Mighty King, lover of justice, you have established equity;
You have executed justice and righteousness in Jacob.
Extol the Lord our God; worship at his footstool. Holy is he!

Moses and Aaron were among his priests; Samuel also was among those who called on his name.
They cried to the Lord, and he answered them.
He spoke to them in the pillar of cloud; they kept his decrees, and the statutes that he gave them.
O Lord our God, you answered them; you were a forgiving God to them, but an avenger of their wrongdoings.
Extol the Lord our God, and worship at his holy mountain; for the Lord our God is holy.

Offerings Sentences
If indeed we are awake, fully awake to God's purpose for our lives, the giving of self becomes central to each day's living. Nothing is deemed to be of greater value than the sharing of God's gifts of love and hope, joy and peace — gifts that have already done their redeeming work in us and which we would see active in the life of friend and neighbor and stranger. Let us share to the full these wonderful gifts of God with others.

Prayer of Dedication
We place this offering, O God, as a sign and seal of our devotion, on this common table, which represents our common purpose in serving you. Guide us in its use, we pray, that it find a redeeming work to do — that persons in need be healed and that many be awakened to the wonder of your love. All that the name of Jesus be exalted and that all of your children be made whole. Amen.

Benediction
When we become fully awake, we shall see Christ clearly. Moreover, we shall see that work, that holy work, which he would have us do as his followers. May this blessing of seeing be ours now — that we go in peace, that we serve the Lord. Amen!

Unity In Christ

Ephesians 4:1-6, 15-16
John 17:20-24

Call to Worship
We gather with sisters and brothers the world over to worship the one God.
We rejoice that we are part of one family, the family of God.
We come to one table, to acknowledge one Lord and Savior.
Here we are strengthened in Christ and united for the journey that is ours together.
We take confidence in Christ's promise, that the Holy Spirit will be with us.
So would we seek the Spirit's presence in this hour and yield to its prompting.

Invocation
Patient and loving God, your will is that we be one — this that we might understand that your love is for all of us, that no one is excluded from your family circle, moreover, that no one should think of self more highly than another. You sent your Son Jesus into our midst to teach us this great lesson, to show by a costly sacrifice of love that we are all welcome at your table, that we indeed find strength in the unity of spirit we affirm at the table. Thus, our words are those of gratitude and praise. You have done for us that which we in our separate ways have consistently failed to do. So with thanksgiving we come — with openness of heart and mind — to learn more and so mature in our understanding and our doing of the faith. May that happen this day, this hour. In Jesus' name. Amen.

Call to Confession
We speak of being one in Christ. Yet barriers still remain — which separate one Christian from the other. These are apparent to any with eyes to see. Christ came that *all* walls of hostility fall, that

there be not separation but unity. In many ways, however, we continue to spurn Christ's sacrifice on our behalf and have instead followed our own personal agendas that divide and keep us strangers to one another's longings and needs. Let us confess this, as with other Christians we approach the table of our Lord.

Prayer of Confession
It is with sadness, O God, that we confess that one of the most broken hours of the week, broken in many ways, is this time of worship on Sunday morning. We must acknowledge, to our shame, that we know few of those sisters and brothers who this very hour worship you in the church down the street. Moreover, if we were pressed to admit it, there are many in our own congregation that we know precious little about. There has not been that sharing of mind to mind, heart to heart, and spirit to spirit. Thus, as we approach the Lord's table, we do not know how to pray on our sister's or brother's behalf, how to pray for the other's well-being. With penitent hearts for this, a grievous shortcoming on our part, we ask your forgiveness. Furthermore, grant us, we pray, a different frame of mind and heart. May the love of Jesus yet work its wondrous power in our midst — healing, reconciling, and making whole. Then there shall be true joy as we gather at the table, with Christ as risen Lord there for us all. It is in his name that we ask this. Amen.

Words of Assurance
Jesus wept over Jerusalem. Jesus weeps today, on each and every occasion when we who bear the name Christian fail to manifest that oneness of heart and spirit that he both announced and lived. Yet Christ's love remains ever present. It is there for all who would call upon it. Christ still labors to make us one in him. Let us rejoice in that!
Thanks be to God, who would have us all grow up in love.

Psalter Reading (Psalm 133)
How very good and pleasant it is when kindred live together in unity!
It is like precious oil on the head,

Running down upon the beard, on the beard of Aaron, running down over the collar of his robes.
It is like the dew of Hermon, which falls on the mountains of Zion.
For there the Lord ordained his blessing,
Life evermore.

Offering Sentences
Christ has set the table with the greatest of all gifts, his own body and blood. Now we come to offer our gifts. Let them flow from the heart as well, the best that we can bring forth — from our devotion, our talents, our thanksgiving. Let them join with gifts of believers from round the world, as together we proclaim the good news: Because Christ lives, we too shall live. In this spirit do we share in our common mission.

Prayer of Dedication
How wonderful to know, O God, that these gifts can be multiplied many times over by your love. For servant hands can take this offering and so route resources to places of dire need, there to be administered with care and compassion, eliciting responses of love from still others of your children. Thus does the story of your reconciling and redeeming work spread — until it shall finally unite us all as one. Thank you, God, for allowing us to have a part in this great work. Amen.

Benediction
Go forth, knowing that you are supported on all sides by sisters and brothers in the faith, indeed a great cloud of witnesses, all of whom look to Jesus, the pioneer and perfecter of our faith, whose strength and purpose and love undergird all that we are and all that we shall do together. Let us all gladly affirm our oneness in him. Amen!

Willingly

Luke 9:51-62
Galatians 5:1, 13-14

Call to Worship
Our Savior consistently sounds the call: "Follow me!"
Excuses will hardly do.
Ours should be nothing less than an enthusiastic: "Yes!"
Yet that can be forced from no one. It must be spontaneous and heartfelt.
In worship this morning, let us once more listen.
And on hearing, let us each determine what our response shall be.

Invocation
God, as close to us as breathing, as majestic as the immense expanse of stars and galaxies, how fortunate we are to be included in your work and fellowship. Because of who you are — the loving, revealing, sharing God — we can know clearly our life's purpose and our role as active participants in that purpose. For you would have us assist in binding harmoniously all things together in the one household of God. Moreover, we know that you value our participation, because you do not force us, but invite us. May our response then be a wholehearted commitment, an eagerness to engage in daily tasks of announcing and living your way, a way of reconciling and making whole things in heaven and things on earth. In the name of him who is with us and who would lead us in this holy way, Jesus the Christ, Guide and Friend. Amen.

Call to Confession
In spite of the fact that God makes us an offer that is foolishness itself to refuse, we nonetheless, it seems, are always ready with excuses. We would postpone full commitment for another, better time, even though our Lord clearly states that *now* is the appropriate moment, *now* the right time, the *best* of all days. Let us assess our response and our needs, as together we bring before God words of confession.

Prayer of Confession

Many are the excuses we offer, heavenly Father, and so do we spurn your invitation to discipleship. We would make following you a lark, rather than a challenge worthy of and demanding our best talents. We place other invitations to this or that ahead of your holy invitation to serve. Just let us complete this other worthwhile endeavor, and *then* we shall come and help you, O God. How easily are our priorities skewed. Moreover, it does seem that we are more comfortable looking back than looking forward. For looking back, all is known; while looking forward, we have to contend with the unknown, and that makes us most uncomfortable. We're hardly venturesome or courageous, even with you by our side. Forgive us these many excuses, Father; help us to push them all aside, that a new day might dawn in our lives, that we become truly the children of God you mean us to be, fully engaged in your work of serving and loving people into wholeness. For this is the Way, and the Truth, and the Life. So do we pray. Amen.

Words of Assurance

How patient is the care and nurture of God. God never forces us, yet is always there to take us by the hand and so guide us past the rough spots. God makes us feel so very wanted, so very much needed to complete the family that God is assembling from the ends of the earth. Let our response be one of gratitude, renewed dedication, and zeal that finds its joy in service.
Praise be to you, O God, for your steadfast love and for your persistence — which is our hope.

Psalter Reading (from Psalm 77)

I will call to mind the deeds of the Lord; I will remember your wonders of old.
I will meditate on all your work, and muse on your mighty deeds.
Your way, O God, is holy. What god is so great as our God?
You are the God who works wonders; you have displayed your might among the peoples.

With your strong arm you redeemed your people, the descendants of Jacob and Joseph.
When the waters saw you, O God, when the waters saw you, they were afraid; the very deep trembled.
The clouds poured out water; the skies thundered; your arrows flashed on every side.
The crash of your thunder was in the whirlwinds; your lightnings lit up the world; the earth trembled and shook.
Your path was through the sea, your path through the mighty waters; yet your footprints were unseen.
You led your people like a flock by the hand of Moses and Aaron.

Offering Sentences
Our offering is not an excuse but an affirmation. It tells the world that we hold our relationship with God to be central to our living; moreover, that it is our desire to participate in God's work in the world. We thus hold nothing back, but give to the full extent of our talents and treasure. Such is our worship of God through the tithes and the offerings that we now bring forward.

Prayer of Dedication
You have a task for each of us, O God, a manner in which we can promote your way of love, reconciliation, and peace — in our neighborhood, that community in which we dwell, and to the far reaches of this earth, of which we may know very little. Just as the gifts we now present are a part of us, so use every other part of us in holy service — that others may find needs answered through the compassionate and faithful hand of one who cares. You will ever provide us with the resources, O God. Let them flow unimpeded through us to others. In Jesus' name. Amen.

Benediction
Away with excuses. God can't *make* us. But we can willingly and joyfully commit ourselves to God's service. That will please God, will bring peace to our lives, and will so inspire our neighbor also to follow the way that leads to life. Amen!

Scripture References

Exodus
34:29-35 — 163

Deuteronomy
26:1-11 — 152
34:1-12 — 159

Joshua
24:1-3a, 14-25 — 31

1 Samuel
17:32-46a, 48-50a — 28

2 Samuel
6:1-5, 11-19 — 43
7:1-14, 17 — 52

Psalter Readings from
Psalm 9 — 29
Psalm 15 — 50
Psalm 16 — 123
Psalm 19 — 114
Psalm 22 — 111
Psalm 23 — 135
Psalm 25 — 35
Psalm 29 — 95
Psalm 30 — 14, 117
Psalm 31 — 86
Psalm 32 — 98
Psalm 34 — 23
Psalm 36 — 144
Psalm 37 — 20
Psalm 47 — 38
Psalm 51 — 129
Psalm 63 — 77
Psalm 65 — 150
Psalm 66 — 47
Psalm 77 — 170
Psalm 78 — 26
Psalm 84 — 53
Psalm 85 — 105
Psalm 86 — 41, 108
Psalm 89 — 59
Psalm 90 — 160
Psalm 95 — 68
Psalm 96 — 17
Psalm 98 — 44, 56
Psalm 99 — 164
Psalm 100 — 153
Psalm 103 — 62
Psalm 104 — 141
Psalm 107 — 80
Psalm 111 — 74
Psalm 112 — 83
Psalm 116 — 89, 147
Psalm 118 — 101, 126
Psalm 119 — 32
Psalm 121 — 121
Psalm 130 — 71
Psalm 133 — 167
Psalm 145 — 138
Psalm 146 — 132, 157

Proverbs
1:20-33 — 88
31 — 92

Isaiah
6:1-8	34
12:2-6	13
35:4-7a	46
42:14-20	22
43:15-21	94
58:9b-14	119

Jeremiah
17:5-10	19

Hosea
6:1-6	155

Amos
5:21-24	31

Micah
5:2-5a	137

Matthew
14:22-33	149
16:13-20	85
18:21-35	61
25:14-30	146
27:3-10	73
27:15-26	128
28:1-10	55

Mark
7:1-9, 14-15, 21-23	49
7:31-37	46
8:31-35	88
8:27-33; 9:2-9	76
10:46-52	22
12:28-34	155
12:41-44	73

Luke
1:39-56	137
2:21-38	16
3:7-18	13
5:1-11	34
6:17-26	19
7:36—8:3	97
9:28-36	163
9:51-62	169
10:25-37	113
13:10-17	119
14:1, 7-14	82
14:25-35	40
16:19-31	131
24:44-53	37

John
2:1-11	143
6:20-31	122
6:24-35	25
6:25-35	152
6:35, 41-51	70
6:56-69	107
10:11-18	134
12:12-19	100
13:1-9	128
13:31-35	91
14:8-17, 25-27	140
14:23-29	104
15:1-8	110
15:9-17	67
17:6-19	79
17:20-24	166
20:19-31	125
21:1-19	116

Romans
6:3-11	55
8:14-17	140
10:14-18	125
13:8-14a	64
14:7-9	159

1 Corinthians
12:1-11	143
13:4-8a, 13	91

2 Corinthians
4:3-6	76
4:13-18	104
5:16-21	94
9:5-15	146

Galatians
5:1, 13-14	169

Ephesians
1:17-23	37
3:14-19	79
4:1-6, 15-16	166
4:7, 11-16	25
4:25—5:2	70
6:1-4	58
6:10-17	107

1 Timothy
6:6-11, 17-19	131

Philemon
1-21	40

Hebrews
13:1-8, 15-16	82

James
1:22-27	49
1:23-25	113
1:25	64

1 Peter
2:4-6	85

1 John
4:16b-21	110